1st EDITION

Perspectives on Diseases and Disorders

Postpartum Depression

Jacqueline Langwith

Book Editor

Detroit • New York • San Francisco • New Haven, Conn • Waterville, Maine • London

GALE
CENGAGE Learning™

Elizabeth Des Chenes, *Managing Editor*

© 2012 Greenhaven Press, a part of Gale, Cengage Learning

Articles in Greenhaven Press anthologies are often edited for length to meet page requirements. In addition, original titles of these works are changed to clearly present the main thesis and to explicitly indicate the author's opinion. Every effort is made to ensure that Greenhaven Press accurately reflects the original intent of the authors. Every effort has been made to trace the owners of copyrighted material.

Cover image © Ian Hooton/Science Photo Library/Alamy

LIBRARY OF CONGRESS CATALOGING-IN-PUBLICATION DATA

Postpartum depression / Jacqueline Langwith, book editor.
   p. cm. -- (Perspectives on diseases and disorders)
Includes bibliographical references and index.
ISBN 978-0-7377-5782-8 (hardback)
1. Postpartum depression--Popular works. I. Langwith, Jacqueline.
RG852.P67 2012
618.7'6--dc23

2011053375

Printed in the United States of America
1 2 3 4 5 6 7 16 15 14 13 12

CONTENTS

CHAPTER 2 Controversies Surrounding
Postpartum Depression

FOREWORD

"Medicine, to produce health, has to examine disease."
—Plutarch

Independent research on a health issue is often the first step to complement discussions with a physician. But locating accurate, well-organized, understandable medical information can be a challenge. A simple Internet search on terms such as "cancer" or "diabetes," for example, returns an intimidating number of results. Sifting through the results can be daunting, particularly when some of the information is inconsistent or even contradictory. The Greenhaven Press series Perspectives on Diseases and Disorders offers a solution to the often overwhelming nature of researching diseases and disorders.

From the clinical to the personal, titles in the Perspectives on Diseases and Disorders series provide students and other researchers with authoritative, accessible information in unique anthologies that include basic information about the disease or disorder, controversial aspects of diagnosis and treatment, and first-person accounts of those impacted by the disease. The result is a well-rounded combination of primary and secondary sources that, together, provide the reader with a better understanding of the disease or disorder.

Each volume in Perspectives on Diseases and Disorders explores a particular disease or disorder in detail. Material for each volume is carefully selected from a wide range of sources, including encyclopedias, journals, newspapers, nonfiction books, speeches, government documents, pamphlets, organization newsletters, and position papers. Articles in the first chapter provide an authoritative, up-to-date overview that covers symptoms, causes and effects, treatments, cures, and medical advances. The second chapter presents a substantial number of opposing viewpoints on controversial treatments and other current debates relating to the volume topic. The third chapter offers a variety of personal perspectives on the disease or disorder. Patients, doctors, caregivers, and loved ones represent just some of the voices found in this narrative chapter.

Each Perspectives on Diseases and Disorders volume also includes:

- An **annotated table of contents** that provides a brief summary of each article in the volume.
- An **introduction** specific to the volume topic.
- Full-color **charts and graphs** to illustrate key points, concepts, and theories.
- Full-color **photos** that show aspects of the disease or disorder and enhance textual material.
- **"Fast Facts"** that highlight pertinent additional statistics and surprising points.
- A **glossary** providing users with definitions of important terms.
- A **chronology** of important dates relating to the disease or disorder.
- An annotated list of **organizations to contact** for students and other readers seeking additional information.
- A **bibliography** of additional books and periodicals for further research.
- A detailed **subject index** that allows readers to quickly find the information they need.

Whether a student researching a disorder, a patient recently diagnosed with a disease, or an individual who simply wants to learn more about a particular disease or disorder, a reader who turns to Perspectives on Diseases and Disorders will find a wealth of information in each volume that offers not only basic information, but also vigorous debate from multiple perspectives.

INTRODUCTION

More Americans were living in poverty in 2010 than at any other time since the US Census Bureau began estimating the poverty rate fifty-two years ago. According to the US Census Bureau, one in six, or 46.2 million, Americans lived in poverty that year. Statistics from the Center for American Progress indicate that a large percentage of these Americans were women, and a large percentage of these women were mothers. Studies suggest that mothers living in poverty face many threats to their physical and emotional health, such as hunger, lack of access to health care, homelessness, domestic violence, and substance abuse. Yet another threat poor women must grapple with is that they are more likely to suffer from postpartum depression than other women.

When new moms are questioned about their mental health, those who are poor are more likely to indicate that they are depressed. For example, in a study published in 2007, researchers at the University of Iowa surveyed more than four thousand women in four Iowa counties who had recently given birth. The women were asked whether they felt sad or hopeless, had trouble concentrating, and other questions the answers to which can help identify depression. Twenty-eight percent of women whose annual incomes were less than ten thousand dollars were identified as having depression compared to just 6.7 percent of women with annual incomes of seventy thousand dollars or more. In addition to low annual income, the researchers found that having less than a college education, having low occupational prestige, being young, being single, and having more than one child are all significant risk factors for postpartum depression. Lisa Segre, one of the authors of the study, explains how childbirth can trigger depression in women already dealing with multiple stressors in their lives. According to Segre, "women who are poor already have a lot of stress, ranging from poor living conditions to concerns about paying the bills. The birth of an infant can represent additional financial and emotional stress, and depression negatively impacts the woman's ability to cope with these already difficult circumstances."

Researchers from the University of Rochester and the University of Pittsburgh also found an association between low income and postpartum depression. In order to check the accuracy of depression screening tools, the researchers interviewed nearly two hundred low-income urban moms. They found that more than half of them met the criteria for a diagnosis of depression at some point between two weeks and fourteen months after giving birth. In a news release announcing their findings in 2010, Linda Chaudron, one of the study's authors, states, "This is an unexpected, very high proportion to meet the diagnostic criteria for depression."

A story that aired on National Public Radio's *All Things Considered* program in 2005 provides a glimpse into the lives of women who struggle with postpartum depression and economic adversity. In the story, commentator Jill Vaughn, a job counselor in upstate New York, describes the plight of three new mothers who were unemployed, lived in poverty, and suffered from postpartum depression. In the excerpt below Vaughn talks about a young mother named Shawnee:

> There's no hall table for mail in Shawnee's apartment, no key rack. The kitchen counter's piled high with bills and coats. In the living room, clothes are folded and stacked against the wall. Shawnee lives with her brother and sister, and their emotional landscape's more cluttered than

the physical one. They were abandoned by their mother, then raised on and off by an abusive father. Anger simmers near the surface. There are infant twins and a toddler to care for. Exhaustion means the house is a mess. Shawnee hasn't been out of the apartment in a week. Her skin is pale, her eyes dull. I see the familiar signs of postpartum depression thriving on isolation and chaos.

Statistics indicate that Shawnee and many other depressed low-income women are often reluctant to seek help. Treatments for postpartum depression include medication, counseling, group therapy, and a combination of these. Practical barriers such as a lack of child care, transportation, or insurance; and social and cultural barriers, such as stigma, beliefs about mental illness, and religious beliefs, have been identified as inhibiting low-income women from seeking treatment. In a 2007 study, researchers Laura S. Abrams and Katrina Dornig of the University of California at Los Angeles found that when

A backer of federal funds to support education, detection, and treatment of postpartum depression, actress Brooke Shields speaks on the issue at a press conference as lawmakers look on. (© AP Images/Susan Walsh)

low-income women in the Los Angeles area were asked what they thought about postpartum depression, many of them expressed beliefs that postpartum depression "didn't exist" or "if you were strong it wouldn't happen to you." They also expressed a fear of telling others about their depressive feelings, thinking that they would be judged, labeled as crazy, considered a bad mother, and rejected.

Postpartum depression is a serious mental disorder that can have tragic consequences if not treated. Increasing awareness of postpartum depression among low-income women and removing barriers to treatment are critical to lessening the impact of this disorder. In *Perspectives on Diseases and Disorders: Postpartum Depression*, the authors discuss the science behind postpartum depression and the extent of scientific knowledge about this disorder. They debate some of the controversial issues surrounding postpartum depression, and those affected by it share their personal stories.

CHAPTER 1

Understanding Postpartum Depression

An Overview of Postpartum Depression

Paula Ford-Martin and Ken Wells

In the following viewpoint Paula Ford-Martin and Ken Wells provide an overview of postpartum depression (PPD), a malady that strikes some mothers soon after their babies are born. According to Ford-Martin and Wells, there are two types of postpartum depression: early onset and late onset. Early-onset PPD is known as the "baby blues." It occurs within the first days and weeks after a baby is born, is relatively mild, generally lasts for a brief period of time, and is very common among new mothers. Depression that afflicts a new mom several weeks after her baby's birth is referred to as late-onset PPD. This type of PPD is more severe, lasts longer, and generally requires treatment. Ford-Martin and Wells are nationally published medical writers.

Photo on previous page. Statistics reveal that low-income mothers are affected more by postpartum depression than women with higher incomes. The lack of affordable medical resources contributes to the problem. (© AJPhoto/Photo Researchers, Inc.)

Postpartum depression, or PPD, affects approximately 15% of all childbearing women. The onset of postpartum depression tends to be gradual and may persist for many months or develop into a second

SOURCE: Paula Ford-Martin and Ken R. Wells, "Postpartum Depression," *Gale Encyclopedia of Alternative Medicine*, 2009. Copyright © 2009, reproduced by permission of Gale, a part of Cengage Learning.

bout following a subsequent pregnancy. Mild to moderate cases are sometimes unrecognized by women themselves. Many women feel ashamed and may conceal their difficulties. This is a serious problem that disrupts women's lives and can have effects on the baby, other children, partners, and other relationships. Levels of depression for fathers can also increase significantly.

Postpartum depression is often divided into two types: early onset and late onset. Early-onset PPD most often seems like the "blues," a mild brief experience during the first days or weeks after birth. During the first week after the birth, up to 80% of mothers experience the "baby blues."

This period is usually a time of extra sensitivity; symptoms include tearfulness, irritability, anxiety, and mood changes, which tend to peak between three to five days after childbirth. The symptoms normally disappear within two weeks without requiring specific treatment apart from understanding, support, skills, and practice. In short, some depression, fatigue, and anxiety may fall within the "normal" range of reactions to giving birth.

FAST FACT

According to Childbirth Connections' 2008 Listening to Mothers II Survey, 63 percent of mothers experience some degree of depressive symptoms within eighteen months after childbirth.

Late-onset PPD appears several weeks after birth. It involves slowly growing feelings of sadness, depression, lack of energy, chronic fatigue, inability to sleep, change in appetite, significant weight loss or gain, and difficulty caring for the baby.

Causes and Symptoms

Experts cannot always say what causes postpartum depression. Most likely, it is caused by a combination of factors that vary from person to person. Some researchers think that women are vulnerable to depression at all major turning points in their reproductive cycle, childbirth being only one of these markers. Factors before the baby's birth

New Mothers Report Feelings of Depression

Based on a survey of women who had given birth anywhere from a few weeks to twelve months earlier.

Have you experienced any of the following in the previous two weeks?

Base: all mothers n=1573	Strongly disagree	Disagree	Neither agree nor disagree	Agree	Strongly agree
Had shifting emotions	26%	15%	10%	27%	21%
Experienced sleep disturbance	32%	19%	6%	25%	17%
Felt anxious about baby	29%	23%	15%	21%	11%
Experienced loss of sense of self	40%	21%	11%	16%	11%
Had mental confusion	43%	19%	12%	17%	9%
Felt guilt about mothering behavior	44%	24%	11%	12%	8%
Had suicidal thoughts	78%	11%	5%	3%	2%

Taken from: Eugene P. Declercq et al. *New Mothers Speak Out*, Childbirth Connection, August 2008.

that are associated with a higher risk of PPD include severe vomiting (hyperemesis), premature labor contractions, and psychiatric disorders in the mother. In addition, new mothers commonly experience some degree of depression during the first weeks after birth. Pregnancy and birth are accompanied by sudden hormonal changes that affect emotions. Additionally, the 24-hour responsibility for a newborn infant represents a major psychological and lifestyle adjustment for most mothers, even after the first child. These physical and emotional stresses are usually accompanied by inadequate rest until the baby's routine stabilizes, so fatigue and depression are not unusual.

In addition to hormonal changes and disrupted sleep, certain cultural expectations appear to place women from those cultures at increased risk of postpartum depression. For example, women who bear daughters in societies with a strong preference for sons (such as Communist China) are at increased risk of postpartum depression. In other cultures, a strained relationship with the husband's family is a risk factor. In Western countries, domestic violence is associated with a higher rate of PPD.

Experiences of PPD vary considerably but usually include several symptoms.

Feelings:
- persistent low mood
- inadequacy, failure, hopelessness, helplessness
- exhaustion, emptiness, sadness, tearfulness
- guilt, shame, worthlessness
- confusion, anxiety, and panic
- fear for the baby and of the baby
- fear of being alone or going out

Behaviors:
- lack of interest or pleasure in usual activities
- insomnia or excessive sleep, nightmares
- not eating or overeating
- decreased energy and motivation
- withdrawal from social contact
- poor self-care
- inability to cope with routine tasks

Thoughts:
- inability to think clearly and make decisions
- lack of concentration and poor memory
- running away from everything
- fear of being rejected by the partner
- worry about harm or death to partner or baby
- ideas about suicide

Some symptoms may not indicate a severe problem. However, persistent low mood or loss of interest or pleasure in activities, along with four other symptoms occurring together for a period of at least two weeks, indicate clinical depression and require adequate treatment.

There are several important risk factors for postpartum depression, including the following:
- stress
- lack of sleep
- poor nutrition
- lack of support from one's partner, family, or friends
- family history of depression
- labor/delivery complications for mother or baby
- premature or postmature delivery
- problems with the baby's health
- separation of mother and baby
- a difficult baby (temperament, feeding, sleeping problems)
- pre-existing neurosis or psychosis

Diagnosis and Treatment

Diagnosis of postpartum depression can be made through a clinical interview with the patient to assess symptoms.

Postpartum depression can be effectively alleviated through counseling and support groups, so that the mother does not feel she is alone in her feelings. Acupuncture, traditional Chinese medicine, yoga, meditation, and herbs can all help the mother suffering from postpartum depression return to a state of balance.

Recommended herbal remedies to ease depressive episodes may include damiana (*Turnera diffusa*), ginseng (*Panax ginseng*), lady's slipper (*Cypripedium calceolus*), lavender (*Lavandula angustifolia*), oats (*Avena sativa*), rosemary (*Rosmarinus officinalis*), skullcap (*Scutellaria laterifolia*), St. John's wort (*Hypericum perforatum*), and vervain (*Verbena officinalis*). Women who are breastfeeding or are suffering from a chronic medical condition should consult a healthcare professional before taking any herbal remedies.

Some strategies that may help new mothers cope with the stress of becoming a parent include:

- Valuing her role as a mother and trusting her own judgment.
- Making each day as simple as possible.
- Avoiding extra pressures or unnecessary tasks.
- Trying to involve her partner more in the care of the baby from the beginning.
- Discussing with her partner how both can share the household chores and responsibilities.
- Scheduling frequent outings, such as walks and short visits with friends.
- Sharing her feelings with her partner or a friend who is a good listener.
- Talking with other mothers to help keep problems in perspective.
- Trying to sleep or rest when the baby is sleeping.
- Taking care of her health and well being.

Antidepression Medications

Several treatment options exist, including medication, psychotherapy, counseling, and group treatment and support strategies, depending on the woman's needs. One effective treatment combines antidepressant medication and psychotherapy. These types of medication are often effective when used for three to four weeks. Any medication use must be carefully considered if the woman is breastfeeding, but with some medications, continuing breastfeeding is safe. There are many classes of antidepression medications. Two of the most commonly prescribed for PPD are selective serotonin reuptake inhibitors (SSRIs) such as citalopram (Celexa), escitalopram (Lexapro), fluoxetine (Prozac), paroxetine (Paxil, Pexeva), and sertraline (Zoloft), and tricyclids, such as amitriptyline (Elavil),

Some researchers report that in addition to experiencing depression following childbirth, women may be vulnerable to depression at all major stages of pregnancy. (© Nic Cleave/Alamy)

desipramine (Norpramin), imipramine (Tofranil), and nortriptyline (Aventyl, Pamelor). Nevertheless, medication alone is never sufficient and should always be accompanied by counseling or other support services. Also, many women with postpartum depression feel isolated. It is important for these women to know that they are not alone in their feelings. There are various postpartum depression support groups available in local communities, often sponsored by non-profit organizations or hospitals. . . .

When a woman has supportive friends and family, mild postpartum depression usually disappears quickly. If depression becomes severe, a mother cannot care for herself and the baby, and in rare cases, hospitalization may be necessary. However, medication, counseling, and support from others usually work to cure even severe depression in three to six months.

Exercise, including yoga, can help enhance a new mother's emotional wellbeing. New mothers should also try to cultivate good sleeping habits and learn to rest when they feel physically or emotionally tired. It is important for a woman to learn to recognize her own warning signs of fatigue and respond to them by taking a break.

Postpartum Depression and Bipolar Disorder

Michele Hoos

In the following viewpoint Michele Hoos discusses the tough treatment decisions faced by pregnant women with bipolar disorder. Generally, bipolar treatment consists of one or more medications that may carry risks to developing fetuses, says Hoos. As a result, many pregnant women with bipolar disorder stop taking their medications. These women, according to Hoos, risk experiencing severe postpartum depression and even psychosis. Hoos says women with bipolar disorder must carefully weigh their own individual risks when deciding whether to discontinue or stay on their medications. Hoos is a multimedia journalist who focuses on health and lifestyle reporting.

As recently as 10 years ago, doctors advised women with bipolar disorder not to have children. While that thinking is now dated, bipolar women often face tough decisions about how to handle their medication during pregnancy.

Most drugs prescribed for bipolar disorder carry some risk of birth defects, yet women who discontinue medication risk relapsing into a manic or depressive episode; during the postpartum phase the relapse rate is as high as 50% to 70%, by some estimates. Even more alarming, bipolar women are 100 times more likely than other women to experience postpartum psychosis, a severe mood disorder that, at its very worst, can result in infanticide.

Sally, 37, started taking lithium after a severe manic episode seven years ago. She eventually switched to other drugs, but in 2007 she stopped her medication altogether when she learned that she was pregnant.

The pregnancy was uneventful. Her daughter, Stella, did arrive six weeks early, but after 21 days in the hospital Stella was finally at home and thriving.

> **FAST FACT**
>
> In a 2008 study of women referred to treatment for postpartum depression, 54 percent were found to have a lifetime diagnosis of bipolar disorder.

Sally, meanwhile, was falling apart. "I was extremely hyperactive," she says. "I was going a million miles an hour." Everyone had told her, "When the baby sleeps, you sleep"—but she couldn't rest. While Stella napped, Sally would clean her Jackson, N.J., home yet again, wiping down doorknobs and light switches. She baked blueberry cobbler at 6 A.M. and pulled weeds into the night.

Though she had restarted her meds the day she gave birth to Stella, after a string of sleepless nights several months later Sally finally realized that lithium was the only thing that would bring her back to her senses. And it did.

Yet Sally continued to have doubts that she was strong enough to be a mother. These are doubts that many women with bipolar disorder share.

Say No to Drugs?

Two years ago, Meredith, 26, of Dix Hills, N.Y., was diagnosed with bipolar disorder and began taking lithium.

Most drugs prescribed for bipolar disorder carry some risk of birth defects. (© Paul Doyle/Alamy)

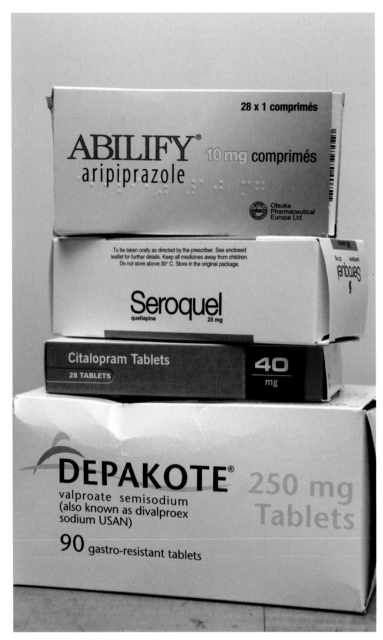

Now she is planning her wedding and, each night, takes a cocktail of mood stabilizers, antidepressants, and antipsychotics: lithium, Abilify, propranolol (Inderal), and escitalopram (Lexapro). "I was grateful for the lithium at first," she says. "But then I was like, 'There go all my options for having kids.'"

When it was first approved by the FDA [Food and Drug Administration] in 1970, lithium was believed to cause heart-valve defects in an extremely high percentage of infants born to mothers who were on the drug (about 1 in 50). Decades later, new research has downgraded the risk, to about 1 in 1,000 to 2,000.

Bipolar medications aren't considered as risky during pregnancy as they once were, but they aren't exactly harmless either. According to the FDA's letter-grade system for drug safety during pregnancy, most psychotropic drugs pose a potential risk to the fetus. Studies have found that the anticonvulsants valproic acid (Depakote) and carbemazepine (Tegretol) can cause birth defects ranging from physical deformities to spina bifida, for instance, while some research suggests that another anticonvulsant, lamotrigine, may carry an increased risk of cleft palate.

The risk of birth defects is small, yet the decision to stop taking medication is common, even among women with severe psychiatric illness. Last year, after she got engaged, and after consulting her psychiatrist, Meredith decided to start tapering off lithium. "I, personally, would like to not be on any medication," she says, when considering a future pregnancy. "I just don't want to take any chances."

Should bipolar women discontinue their medication? According to reproductive psychiatrist Catherine Birndorf, the founding director of the Payne Whitney Women's Program at New York Presbyterian Hospital, "There's not just one answer." The severity of bipolar disorder varies widely from person to person, and for this reason it's difficult to standardize care for pregnant women with the disorder, Dr. Birndorf explains. "Each case must be considered on an individual basis," she says.

But what many of Dr. Bindorf's patients do not initially realize is that untreated illness—and not just medication—can be risky. According to a 2007 study in the *American Journal of Psychiatry*, women who discontinued mood stabilizers during pregnancy spent over 40% of their pregnancy in an "illness episode." And research suggests that the effects of maternal depression on the fetus can lead to complications both during and after pregnancy.

Still, many bipolar women believe they have to stop taking all of their medications for the sake of their child—and often psychiatrists or OB/GYNs steer women away from medication, according to Margaret Spinelli, director of the Women's Program in Psychiatry at Columbia University.

"I hope that women will come to a perinatal psychiatrist to get an evaluation," says Dr. Spinelli. "Because they

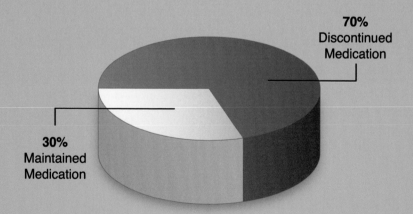

Most Women with Bipolar Disorder Discontinue Medication During Pregnancy

70%
Discontinued
Medication

30%
Maintained
Medication

Based on a study of eighty-nine women with bipolar disorder recruited at the Perinatal and Reproductive Psychiatry Clinical Research Program at Massachussetts General Hospital.

Taken from: Adele C. Viguera, et al. "Risk of Recurrence in Women with Bipolar Disorder During Pregnancy: Prospective Study of Mood Stabilizer Discontinuation." *American Journal of Psychiatry*, December 2007.

can become so ill. And the problem is that if they become really ill during the pregnancy off the medication, it may take a lot more medication to stabilize them."

Postpartum Planning

A complication-free pregnancy with or without medication doesn't mean a woman is in the clear. For any bipolar mother, the trickiest time is not the pregnancy itself but the postpartum period.

Postpartum difficulties are not limited to bipolar women, of course. Many women experience the crying episodes known as the "baby blues," and an estimated 10% of women go through a more severe postpartum depression. Women with bipolar disorder are at much higher risk, however; postpartum psychosis—which is believed to be a form of bipolar disorder—occurs in as many as 25% to 50% of deliveries.

While postpartum psychosis is a serious risk, it's a risk that can be treated, and often prevented, with medication. It's extremely important for a woman with bipolar disorder to have a plan in place with her family and her doctors in the event that she does become psychotic, says Dr. Spinelli. Due to the high risk of psychosis, bipolar women should "really start medicines at least before they deliver," she adds.

As the field of perinatal psychiatry grows, many bipolar women are choosing to stay on medications to avoid any chance of postpartum psychosis or manic episodes. "I'd heard so many horror stories of people harming the baby," says Michele Noll, 37, of Atlanta, who has delivered two healthy babies while taking mood stabilizers.

"I did not have mood swings," Noll says of her pregnancy and postpartum period. "Nobody even knew I was bipolar."

Breast-feeding presents another challenge. Even though some medications are safe while nursing, feeding a baby requires waking up often throughout the night. And in people with bipolar disorder, sleep deprivation can trigger a manic episode.

Shanun Carey, 25, of Manchester, N.H., became so manic while breast-feeding that she was "bouncing off the walls," eventually volunteering to clean her neighbors' apartments to burn off excess energy. When her daughter was six months old, Carey realized she had to stop breast-feeding to get healthy again; she switched to formula so she could resume her medications and a regular sleep schedule.

Formula isn't the only solution. Rachael Bender, 30, of Naples, Fla., who writes a blog called *My Bipolar Pregnancy*, realized that losing sleep would be a huge challenge in trying to breast-feed. But she did want to try, so she and her husband worked out a system when her daughter was an infant. To save Bender from getting the baby up and back to sleep, her husband slept in the guest room, next to the bassinet, and brought the baby in to Bender when the baby was hungry. "The hardest thing about the whole pregnancy," Bender says, "was the sleep after she was born."

The Next Generation

Sally, who lapsed into depression after the lithium got her mania under control, still struggles with the ups and downs of bipolar disorder. Because she is committed to being a great parent to Stella, she has made what she says is the most difficult decision of her life.

"Absolutely, I will not have another baby," Sally says, acknowledging that no matter how many times her healthy daughter kisses her, or her husband tells her she's a wonderful mother, she still has doubts related to her bipolar disorder and the amount of attention it requires. "I want to be the best mother I can be, and if I had two children I'd worry that I was spreading myself too thin," she says.

Meredith knows that pregnancy will be "a difficult time," and people have already questioned her decision to have children; a family friend even told her that it would be a "heartache" for her if she did have a child with bipolar disorder. Bipolar disorder does tend to run in families: Studies show that a person is 10 times more likely to develop the disorder if a parent is bipolar.

None of this has swayed Meredith's desire to be a mother.

"I'm not going to *not* have a child because I'm afraid they're going to be bipolar," says Meredith. "I've seen so many wonderful things and I've done so many wonderful things, and I plan to do a lot more. My kid will have a better life than a lot of kids out there. This isn't going to stop me."

The Possibility of a Postpartum Depression Gene

John J. Medina

In the following article John J. Medina provides an overview of research suggesting that there may be a postpartum depression gene. According to Medina, a gene that makes a cellular protein receptor that binds to the neurotransmitter GABA (gamma-aminobutyric acid), may be the cause of postpartum depression. Medina says that in most women, the levels of this receptor go down during pregnancy but return to normal levels after childbirth. In women who suffer from postpartum depression, however, the receptor levels do not rebound after childbirth. Medina says more research needs to be done, but the identification of a postpartum gene provides hope for more effective postpartum depression treatments. Medina is a developmental molecular biologist at the University of Washington School of Medicine, the director of the Brain Center for Applied Learning Research at Seattle Pacific University, and the author of a series of books called *Brain Rules*.

SOURCE: John J. Medina, "Is There a Gene for Postpartum Depression," *Psychiatric Times*, December, 2008, pp. 44–45.

The transition to parenthood is filled to the brim with behavioral extremes. Parents who are otherwise emotionally stable are in one moment thrilled and happier than they have ever been and confused and fearful the next. A friend of mine once theorized that these reactions occur because "parenting is an amateur sport" played by persons who are highly motivated to do the right thing but who often have no idea what that right thing is.

For some couples, the transition to parenthood is not filled with this rich mixture of great perplexity and great joy. For them, parenthood is mostly filled with sadness and even despair. Postpartum depression was originally coined to describe this experience in the mother, although it is becoming clear that fathers can experience very similar emotions too.

Is there a molecular basis for postpartum depression —at least for the type that mothers experience? Recent findings, which I describe here, may answer this question. First, we will focus on several background behavioral and molecular issues and then move on to some interesting data about births in genetically manipulated laboratory animals. . . .

Postpartum Depression

As you know, the probability of experiencing major depression is twice as high in women as it is in men, and pregnancy does not buffer against this risk. Postpartum depression afflicts about 20% of mothers. Higher rates are seen in adolescent mothers than in older mothers.

Mental health professionals who are considering treatment for a depressed pregnant patient must make choices that can be particularly troublesome. Many clinicians are concerned about the potentially damaging effects of antidepressant medications on the developing fetus. Should a woman be treated during pregnancy? As I have discussed

... before, serotonin plays a dramatic role in gestational brain development, especially in the thalamus. Concerns about serotonin's effects on brain development actually held up the FDA's [US Food and Drug Administration's] approval of fluoxetine [e.g., Prozac].

This risk is also observable after parturition [childbirth]. If depression remains untreated, the risk of drug and alcohol abuse and suicide and infanticide greatly increases. Yet, psychotropic drugs may expose a breast-fed baby to these medications. Are there risks associated with this exposure? The possibility of adverse consequences is not zero, although there is a critical need for further research in this area. As if pregnancy were not complicated enough, balancing the risk of potential behavioral consequences of depression with the pharmacological risk of treatment is quite challenging indeed.

There is increasing evidence that men can also experience depression after the birth of their child. The rates can be astonishingly high—about 1 in 4 fathers are affected in some studies; this rate climbs to 1 in 2 if his spouse is also depressed. The effect can be recursive. Loss of emotional support from the female because of depression may cause or exacerbate depression in the male, which in turn may retrigger depressive behaviors in the female.

Depression is a big deal for some families in the transition to parenthood; it is thus gratifying to report some very promising findings regarding its molecular underpinnings. We need only one more piece of background information, which involves a very particular animal model of depression, to understand it fully.

Molecular Background of Human Depression

The literature that reviews the molecular processes in human depression often focuses on the seminal roles of catecholamines and indoleamines [brain chemicals, called

There is increasing evidence that men can also experience depression after childbirth. (© **Bubbles Photography/Alamy**)

neurotransmitters, that relay messages]. Over the years, it has become increasingly clear that other neurotransmitter systems can also mediate the pathogenesis of depression, notably glutamate and GABA [gamma-aminobutyric acid]. One of GABA's attendant receptors plays a prominent role in our story.

Often contrasted with glutamate (the canonical excitatory neurotransmitter), GABA is characterized as the brain's classic "inhibitory" neurotransmitter. Glutamate and GABA function together as a kind of molecular yin-yang by regulating neuronal activity throughout the CNS [central nervous system]. GABA mediates its effects by binding to 1 of 3 transmembrane receptors in specific neurons in the brain (awkwardly called "GABAergic" cells). The binding results in the opening of ion channels, creating a localized increase in the negativity across the plasma membrane. This hyperpolarization of the cell (as opposed to depolarization, which results in a more equal distribution of charge across the membrane) produces the inhibitory effect.

GABA is not always inhibitory. Most of its electrical effects depend on localized current flow in adult cells and even the stage of the development of the cell. In neonatal tissues, GABA acts as an excitatory neurotransmitter and makes a change in its job description only as the tissues mature.

As noted, GABA exerts its effects by binding to 1 of 3 members of the GABA receptor family: $GABA_A$, $GABA_B$, and $GABA_C$. $GABA_A$ and $GABA_B$ are ionotropic receptors. As their name implies, these receptors function directly as the ion channels. $GABA_C$ opens ion channels in a less direct fashion. A classic metabotropic [cell surface] receptor, $GABA_C$ is [gamma] protein-coupled and participates in a signal transduction process that eventually results in the opening of other ion channels. These proteins are complex structures that are composed of smaller subunit proteins (the $GABA_A$ receptor has one called the "subunit," which will be important to our story).

Before we get started on the data, it might be useful to go over one last critical issue. Over the years, a number of animal models have been used to increase our understanding of the molecular substrates undergirding developmental processes. Although there have been a fair number of animal models that mimic aspects of human anxiety disorders, relatively few can be reliably used in the study of human depression.

34

One of the animal tests that is used often involves creating standardized depressive behavior in mice using the Porsolt forced swim test. Another test involves measuring anhedonia, in which the ability to experience pleasure from normally pleasurable activities is inhibited. Both were deployed in the data that I will describe next.

The Data

The researchers decided to focus on the $GABA_A$ receptor for an important reason: the $GABA_A$ receptor is one of the principal targets for the action of many neuroactive products of steroid hormones that are usually called "neurosteroids."

Altered neurosteroid levels have been associated with a wide variety of psychiatric illnesses, including premenstrual syndrome and postpartum depression. A large increase in levels of progesterone-derived neurosteroids occurs during pregnancy, then levels decline rapidly after birth. Understanding how these levels interact with the $GABA_A$ receptor biology turned out to be an important area of inquiry.

The researchers noticed that $GABA_A$ receptor expression was greatly attenuated in the hippocampus of female mice during pregnancy. The loss of the receptor mediated a change in the electrical properties of the tissue, which was demonstrated by whole-cell, patch-clamp recordings (patch-clamp involves using electrodes to record currents in single neurons). Researchers also noticed that this effect was reversed in the postpartum period. The levels of the $GABA_A$ receptor rapidly returned to baseline after the females had given birth.

Knocking Out the $GABA_A$

How would an animal behave if it did not have this receptor or at least one of its subunits? If baseline levels could not ever return in these animals, would they exhibit depressive-like symptoms?

A Gene for Postpartum Depression

Shown below are experiments that may link expression of the γ-aminobutyric acid (GABA) receptor with depressive symptoms, at least in mice. The first panel shows unmanipulated control animals. The second panel shows animals whose GABA receptor has been "knocked out." The third panel shows the same knockout animals; however, they have now been treated with the GABA receptor–subunit agonist, 4,5,6,7-tetrahydroisoxazolo(5,4-c)pyridin-3-ol (THIP).

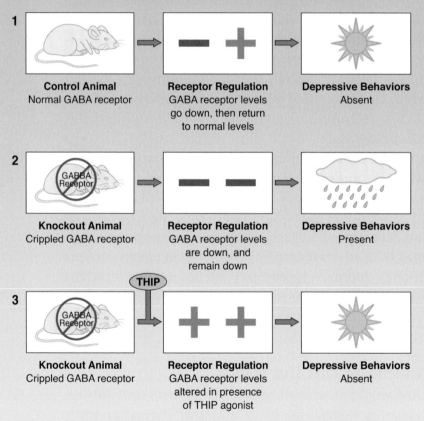

1

Control Animal
Normal GABA receptor

Receptor Regulation
GABA receptor levels
go down, then return
to normal levels

Depressive Behaviors
Absent

2

Knockout Animal
Crippled GABA receptor

Receptor Regulation
GABA receptor levels
are down, and
remain down

Depressive Behaviors
Present

3

THIP

Knockout Animal
Crippled GABA receptor

Receptor Regulation
GABA receptor levels
altered in presence
of THIP agonist

Depressive Behaviors
Absent

Taken from: John Medina. "Is There A Gene for Postpartum Depression?" *Psychiatric Times*, December 2008.

One way to answer this question would be to create knock-out mice that are raised without GABA$_A$. Knock-out mice are genetically engineered to develop without a particular genetic sequence. They present the researcher with a site-specific loss of function. Hints as to the functioning of the knocked-out gene sequence can be obtained simply by noting abnormalities in the function or behavior of the animal.

It is a risky procedure. Some genes are so critical to gestational progress that their disruption results in the death of the animal, often in utero. The researchers knocked out only the subunit we discussed previously. Without this subunit, receptor function is crippled. Happily, the animals survived.

The researchers were able to show depressive symptoms in the knockout mice after birth. After the administration of the standardized Porsolt and anhedonia tests mentioned previously, the animals exhibited robust depressive characteristics. There was a disturbingly large increase in the overall pup mortality in this population. The manipulated mothers were much more likely to neglect or cannibalize their pups compared with unmanipulated littermate controls.

The last series of experiments involved the use of 4,5,6,7-tetrahydro-isoxazolo(5,4-c)pyridin-3-ol (mercifully shortened to THIP, also called "gaboxadol"). This drug, which was first characterized as a sedative, has an extraordinary property: it is a specific GABA$_A$ receptor–subunit receptor agonist. THIP can fully restore GABA$_A$ receptor function, even in an animal that has lost its utility because of a subunit knock-out.

When these animals were treated with THIP, the depressive behaviors measured by the standardized tests and maternal behavior toward the pups vanished, and normal behavior was observed. The presence of functioning GABA$_A$ receptors appeared to be the independent variable in these experiments. Keep them present and normal behavior was observed. Reduce their levels (and inhibit their ability to reestablish themselves) and depression returns. You can turn it on and off like a light switch.

A Gene for Postpartum Depression

Could these data be used to explain postpartum depression? They certainly suggest compelling new lines of research. Remember that it is normal for elevated levels of progesterone-derived neurosteroids to down-regulate $GABA_A$ receptor concentrations during pregnancy and then to reestablish themselves after birth. Could postpartum depression in women be understood as an inability for these receptors to bounce back after birth? If so, it might be possible to test for such a lack of restoration with noninvasive imaging technologies. Is it possible that mutations in the receptor or in molecular moieties, which regulate receptor number, prevent their reestablishment to prepregnancy levels? Could these mutations predict depressive experiences? If so, the isolation of the first gene for postpartum depression might actually be in hand. Using THIP or its derivatives as a possible treatment, there may even be some hope for pharmacological intervention. Promising data indeed, but only promising.

> **FAST FACT**
>
> In a study published in 2011, researchers from Switzerland found that postpartum depression may be linked to low levels of oxytocin, sometimes referred to as the "love hormone."

My usual objections about applying animal research to human behavior hold here, certainly. The mouse cortex is, after all, about the size of a postage stamp, while the human cortex is about the size of a baby blanket. Compelling as these data are, they only suggest areas for human research directions.

These data do not solve the most common nature/nurture issues that dog most behavioral research like this, of course. It is especially important for affective disorders. Data suggest that the relative risk for depression is two-thirds environmental and one-third genetic. Because fathers can also experience depression, which can profoundly influence the spouse, that also must be factored in and perhaps saddled with more weight than other environmental influences.

None of these objections are deal killers. These data may point to the presence of a chromosomal abnormality as a risk factor for depression. It would then suggest that unusually close attention should be paid to any mother who has the chromosomal risk factor. These data may ultimately explain why the transition to parenthood (amateur sport that it is), although never easy for anyone, can be so catastrophically overwhelming to some.

Brain Changes Are Linked to Postpartum Depression

Madonna Behen

In the following article Madonna Behen discusses the findings of researchers studying the brains of women with postpartum depression. According to Behen, researchers found that when women with postpartum depression respond to emotional cues their brains look different in magnetic resonance imaging (MRI) scans than the brains of women who are not suffering from the disease. The research reveals that women with postpartum depression may have difficulty processing their own emotions and responding to the emotions of others. Behen is a health writer. She has written for HealthDay, Woman's Day, and Good Housekeeping magazines.

W omen with postpartum depression have differences in brain functioning that may interfere not only with how they process their own emotions, but also with their ability to be responsive to the emotions of their infants, new research suggests.

SOURCE: Madonna Behen, "Brain Anomalies Found in Moms with Postpartum Depression," *Health Day News*, Septmeber 16, 2010. www.healthday.com. Copyright © 2010 by Health Day News. All rights reserved. Reproduced by permission.

In a small study that involved MRI [magnetic resonance imaging] brain scans, researchers at the University of Pittsburgh Medical Center revealed that women with postpartum depression [PDD] have reduced activity in parts of the brain that control emotional responses and recognize emotional cues in others.

A Brain Basis for Emotional Difficulties of PPD Women

"Our study provides a brain basis for what has been described in clinical settings and behavioral studies, which is that women with postpartum depression may have reduced activity in regions of the brain that process emotions and that are involved in being attuned to others' emotions," said study author Dr. Eydie L. Moses-Kolko, an assistant professor of psychiatry at the University of

A magnetic resonance imaging slide shows the emotional activity zone (in yellow and pink) in the frontal lobe of the human brain. Researchers report that women with postpartum depression show reduced activity in parts of the brain that control emotional responses. (© James Cavallini/Photo Researchers, Inc.)

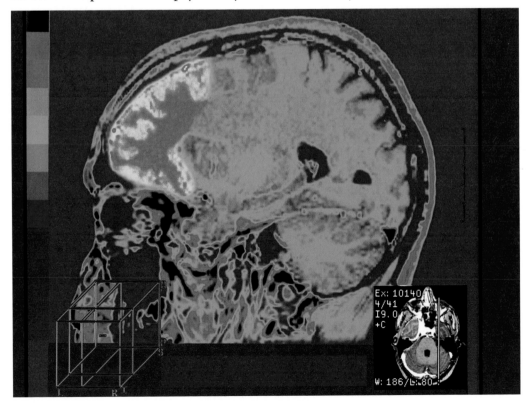

Pittsburgh School of Medicine. These brain abnormalities may help explain why mothers with postpartum depression often have problems bonding with their infants, she noted.

Postpartum depression, which affects an estimated 15 percent of new moms, is different than the typical "baby blues" that often occur after delivery, when a new mother may burst into tears at the drop of a hat, experts said.

While the baby blues usually go away within two weeks of giving birth, postpartum depression can continue for months and often causes such strong feelings of sadness, anxiety or despair that a woman has trouble coping

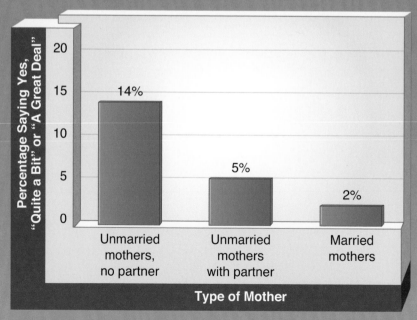

Unmarried Mothers Report More Emotional Problems than Married Mothers

Have emotional problems interfered with your ability to take care of your baby in the first two months after giving birth?

Taken from: Eugene R. Declercq et al. *New Mothers Speak Out.* Childbirth Connection, August 2008.

with her daily tasks. Previous research has shown that maternal depression can negatively affect an infant's mental and physical development.

Moses-Kolko and her colleagues studied 14 depressed and 16 healthy mothers, all of whom delivered a healthy term infant in the preceding 12 weeks, were medication-free and had previously given birth to another child. The mothers were shown images of angry and scared faces, and the researchers examined their neural reactions to the pictures with the use of MRI scans. The mothers also filled out questionnaires that assessed their attachment quality, hostility and pleasure in interaction with their infants.

> **FAST FACT**
>
> According to the 2008 *New Mothers Speak Out* national survey results, about one-third of mothers reported that their postpartum emotional health interfered at least "some" with their ability to care for their baby.

The researchers found that negative emotional faces activated the left dorsomedial prefrontal cortex, which is a social cognition region of the brain, significantly less in depressed mothers than in healthy mothers. Deficits in this region, they said, might represent diminished awareness of the emotions of others and less empathy for them. Another key finding was that when the women saw negative images, communication between the left dorsomedial prefrontal cortex and the left amygdala was present in healthy moms but not in the depressed ones, suggesting that this might be an important neural circuit that regulates emotional response to unpleasant sounds, such as a baby's cry. . . .

Moses-Kolko said more research is needed "to determine what brain patterns are predictive of response to an array of treatments including psychotherapy, medications or hormones."

"This is a very interesting study, but it's really just the beginning," said Michael W. O'Hara, a professor of psychology at the University of Iowa in Iowa City, who specializes in perinatal depression. "More studies need to be done in a much larger sample of women, to see if the results can be replicated."

O'Hara added: "It's my belief that postpartum depression is a heterogeneous disorder that includes depression that is coincidental with childbirth, and depression that is inextricably related to it." Future MRI studies need to differentiate between these two groups of women, he said, because "if we mix these two samples together, it may obscure the true findings."

CHAPTER 2

Controversies Surrounding Postpartum Depression

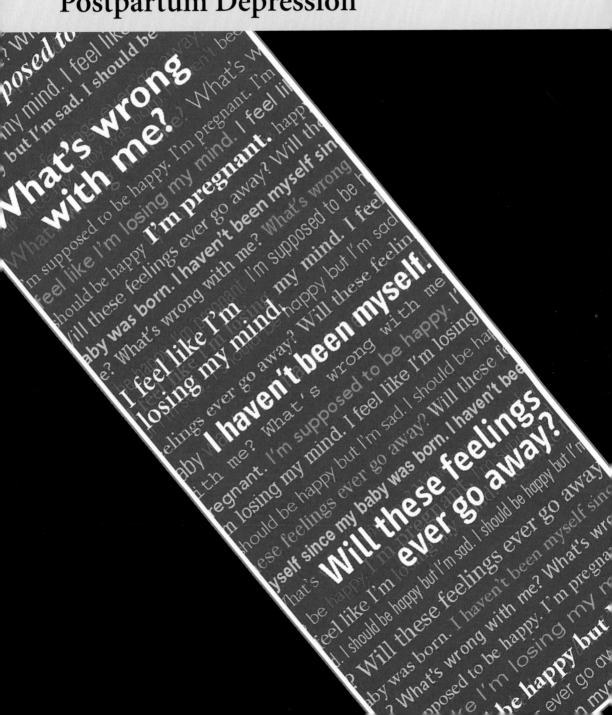

Postpartum Depression Screening Is Necessary

John Grohol

In the following viewpoint John Grohol contends that screening pregnant women for postpartum depression, as provided for in the Melanie Blocker-Stokes MOTHERS Act, is necessary. The MOTHERS Act became law on March 23, 2010, when the legislation was signed by President Barack Obama as part of the health reform law, i.e., the Patient Protection and Affordable Care Act. Before its enactment, the need for the MOTHERS Act was debated, particularly its provisions regarding the screening of pregnant women for postpartum depression. In this viewpoint Grohol takes psychiatrist J. Douglas Bremner to task for saying that there is no evidence to show that mothers are at risk for postpartum depression. According to Grohol, there is ample evidence to show that mothers are at risk for the disease, and screening is necessary to help them before their symptoms become overwhelming. Grohol is the owner and operator of *Psych Central*, an independent mental health and psychology network available on the Internet.

Photo on previous page. New York State's Department of Health is providing information on postpartum depression as part of a public awareness campaign. Ads are being placed on bus benches and in shelters and are also being broadcast on TV and radio.
(© AP Images/NYS Health Department)

SOURCE: John Grohol, "Bremner's False Claims About Postpartum Depression," *Psych Central*, July 15, 2009. www.psychcentral.com. Copyright © 2009 by Psych Central. Reproduced by permission.

Psychiatrist J. Douglas Bremner has weighed in on the Melanie Blocker Stokes MOTHERS Act, [a federal legislative] . . . effort to provide voluntary screenings to pregnant women to help identify postpartum depression before it becomes overwhelming. I'll let Bremner speak for himself:

> The problem with this is the attitude that being a mother is a risk factor for a psychiatric disorder. First of all, there is no evidence that women without a prior history of anxiety and depression have any increased risk of getting post partum depression. So to screen all moms as if giving birth is a risk factor for depression is ridiculous.

My BS alert goes off whenever someone tries to change the argument from a reasonable effort to help increase education and information about a stigmatized mental health issue, to hyperbole, suggesting that a piece of legislation is trying to turn motherhood into a psychiatric disorder. It goes off again when a professional makes an extraordinary claim like, "there is *no evidence* that women without a prior history of anxiety and depression have any increased risk of getting post partum [sic] depression." Really? *Absolutely no evidence?* That's quite a strong statement, and easily proven false with a literature review.

Women Without History of Anxiety or Depression Are Also at Risk of PPD

Where shall we begin? (I have limited space and you have a limited attention span, so I'll just highlight a few studies. . . .)

[L.E.] Ross & [C.] Dennis, for instance, in a literature review found that both substance use and current or past experiences of abuse are associated with increased risk for postpartum depression (PPD).

In urban South African women, [P.G.] Ramchandani and colleagues found the strongest predictors of postnatal depression were exposure to extreme societal stressors

President Barack Obama signs the Health Insurance Reform Bill on March 23, 2010. The bill provides for the screening of women for postpartum depression. (© Pat Benic/UPI/Landov)

(e.g., witnessing a violent crime/danger of being killed) and reporting difficulties with their partner.

[E.] Robertson et al., in a large meta-analysis of research to-date, found that a previous history of depression and anxiety (not just during pregnancy) was predictive of postpartum depression. But they also found that simply experiencing a stressful life event during pregnancy or low levels of social support (e.g., not having any emotional support from your friends or family) could also lead to postpartum depression.

[C.T.] Beck's meta-analysis of 84 studies found:

13 significant predictors of postpartum depression: prenatal depression, self-esteem, childcare stress, prenatal
anxiety, life stress, social support, marital relationships,
depression history, infant temperament, maternity blues,
marital status, SES, and unplanned/unwanted pregnancy.
10 of the 13 risk factors had moderate effect sizes while 3
predictors had small effect sizes.

Look at all of those factors which are *not* depression or
anxiety—I count 9. Even if 3 of those are small-effect size
factors, that still leaves 6 factors which are not depression
or anxiety.

Screening Is Worth It

What about the argument that if depressed women are the
most at-risk, we should simply focus on them?

[J.] Ingram & [J.] Taylor found it wasn't just a woman's
pre-birth depression severity that was important—poor
emotional support and women who had more negative
descriptions of their own childhood were additional risk
factors that played a role in increased risk for postpartum
depression. Who's going to screen for these things, the obstetrician?

Well, no, because the obstetrician is already not doing a
good job at screening for postpartum depression, even in
high-risk women. [D.C.] Hatton et al. found that, among
high-risk women, obstetric care providers may be over-
looking up to one fifth of women with current major depression. Not exactly great numbers there.

If obstetric care providers can't deal with the obvious
cases, I can only imagine how well they do with the more
complex or less obvious ones.

[C.] Monk et al. sums the state of our knowledge on
PPD:

Depression is relatively common during the perinatal period. Approximately 8.5–11% of women experience either a major or minor depression during pregnancy. Nearly 20% of women have a minor or major depression in the first 3 months following delivery.

So up to 1 in 5 women have depression after giving birth, and this isn't something worth noting or screening for? (For comparison's sake, 1 in 10 men and women in the general population might have depression at any given time.) Giving birth doubles your risk of depression, and this isn't an issue? Amazing.

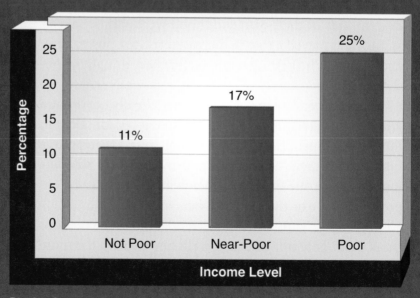

Incidence of Maternal Depression Higher for Poor Women

Percent of mothers with a nine-month-old infant who are moderately or severely depressed:

Taken from: Center on the Developing Child at Harvard University. Maternal Depression Can Undermine the Development of Young Children. Working Paper 8, December 2009.

But don't just take my word for it. [M.L.] Zajicek-Farber's study conducted on high-risk women for postpartum depression concluded that:

> These findings provide additional supportive evidence that more efforts are needed to identify and assess women's depressive symptoms to promote health and safety of young children.

These are *objective researchers* calling for more screenings. Not politicians. And not people (or professionals) with a political agenda.

Now, I understand Bremner's point—let's not *medicalize* and *catastrophize* ordinary motherhood. I agree. And of course a woman's pre-birth depression or anxiety is strongly correlated to postpartum depression. But not exclusively, as Bremner claims.

Bremner claims, with no evidence, that *all mental health screenings* are simply pharmaceutical sales tactics to help increase prescriptions. That's ridiculous. When I worked in community mental health, we ran annual mental health screenings in the clinic—with no funding from any pharmaceutical company—because it *reduces stigma, decreases misinformation and increases education* about mental health issues in the general population.

Mothers Are an "At-Risk" Population

Sorry, but most people don't have time to keep up with a dozen blogs or read monthly journals on the latest research in mental health. Most people know what they know about mental health largely through mainstream media, or their own first-hand experiences with an issue. How is the promotion of *more* information and education about mental health issues a bad thing?

Bremner uses teens as an example of screening gone wrong, but conveniently fails to mention the facts about teenagers and mental health. Teens are an "at-risk" population, hence the reason they are sometimes targeted for screenings. Teens are notorious for being limited in their treatment options (especially in the U.S., where their treatment may be covered by their family's health insurance, meaning a talk with their parents about their mental health issues), and for peer pressure limiting their ability to accept or seek help. (Yes, sorry, if you're seeing a therapist for depression as a teen, you're typically not seen as a "cool" kid.)

Sadly, whether people want to admit it or not, mothers are another "at risk" population. Why? Because society has told mothers time and time again that giving birth is supposed to be a joyous, happy occasion. If you're depressed after giving birth to a child, there must be something wrong with you. Don't draw attention to yourself or your problems. Just try and deal with it, try and take care of the baby, and make it through each day. Mothers don't know they might have something recognized as postpartum depression, much less that they can talk to someone about these feelings or that there's treatment—psychotherapy or medication—readily available for it.

FAST FACT

According to the American Academy of Pediatrics, every year more than four hundred thousand infants are born to mothers who are depressed.

So respectfully, I disagree with Bremner's assessment of the MOTHERS act and its need in today's society. And if you're not going to bother to do the legwork and just make general (false) pronouncements about what the research actually shows (or worse, suggest that *all research that disagrees with you must be in pharma's pocket*), then that's a lazy person's argument. There are too many logical fallacies at work here to list, so I'll just suggest that I expect more reasoned and professional arguments—based upon the actual research—about such important legislation.

Psych Central continues to support the Melanie Blocker Stokes MOTHERS Act because the research shows it would help in the efforts to increase education and correct mis-information about postpartum depression.

Postpartum Depression Screening Is Not Beneficial

K.L. Carlson

In the following viewpoint K.L. Carlson argues that the March 23, 2010, MOTHERS Act, which promotes postpartum depression screening, is not beneficial to women. Carlson believes that postpartum depression is a made-up disorder and not a real mental illness. The MOTHERS Act, she says, is just a way to get more women to take harmful antidepressants and increase the profits of psychiatrists and drug makers. Carlson believes that women should not be fearful of postpartum depression, but they should be fearful of antidepressant medications. Carlson is a former pharmaceutical sales representative. She is the author of *Diary of a Legal Drug Dealer*, *One Drug Rep. Dares to Tell You the Truth* and has been featured in the documentary films *Prescription for Death* and *Making a Killing*.

M om's Opportunity to Access Health, Education, Research, and Support for Postpartum Depression Act sounds very supportive of new mothers.

The truth is just the opposite. The cleverly worded title can be shortened to the Mothers Act and it was written by and for the pharmaceutical industry. It was introduced by Senator Robert Menendez of New Jersey; the state with the most pharmaceutical companies' headquarters. According to the public interest group, Common Cause, Senator Menendez received over $2 million from the healthcare industry, including drug companies.

The Mothers Act was included in the immense health plan that was recently signed into law [March 23, 2010]. New mothers need to be made aware that this Act was not written to benefit them, but to benefit the drug companies. This Act will have grave results—for some mothers literally.

Painting Motherhood as a Mental Illness

Postpartum depression, as defined in the Act, is a "mood disorder" that has three categories. The most severe category is "postpartum psychosis." Notice the use of psychiatric terms. The public is supposed to believe that motherhood can cause mental illness. Fear of a new mother suffering "postpartum psychosis" is then increased

Opponents of the MOTHERS Act's postpartum depression provisions in the federal health care reform bill note the assertion of advocacy group Common Cause that New Jersey senator Robert Menendez (pictured) supported the act because he received over $2 million in contributions from the health care industry, including drug companies in his state. (© AP Images/ Harry Hamburg)

by the Act stating that one in every one thousand new mothers will suffer the mental illness.

The Act states that postpartum depression goes undiagnosed and untreated due to "social stigma surrounding depression and mental illness." So giving birth and becoming a new mother with vastly fluctuating hormones and physiological changes, as well as the demands of a new baby, is now a mental illness. What is the probability the Mothers Act would have been written if psychiatric drugs did not reap more than $330 billion dollars a year?

The Act establishes federally funded grants to screen all new mothers before they leave their birthing centers and to continue screening during the first year. Although it is unknown why some women suffer depression after giving birth, and most likely there are many reasons including concerns of financially supporting a new baby, the pharmaceutical industry has ensured that it is considered a mental illness that will lead to non-curing, addictive, dangerous psychiatric drugs. As stated in the Act, "the new mother shall be referred to an appropriate mental healthcare provider."

"There is no evidence that any mental disorder is caused by chemical imbalance," a Surgeon General's report states. The much-touted idea of brain chemical imbalance is a total myth with no scientific research ever supporting it. All psychiatric "disorders" are voted into existence by the American Psychiatric Association and have no objective diagnostic tests, such as blood tests or hormone tests. The Mothers Act is the latest version of the old story of the Emperor's New Clothes—get people to believe something exists when in fact it does not. Mothers who have trouble emotionally after giving birth do not have any mental illness. They may have temporary

FAST FACT

In 2005–2008, 11 percent of US adults reported taking a prescription antidepressant in the past month, and women were more than twice as likely as men to take them (16 percent compared with 6 percent), according to the US Centers for Disease Control and Prevention.

hormonal imbalance. They may need a stronger emotional support system to feel confident they can get help with the new baby. They may need financial assistance. But they are not mentally ill.

Antidepressant Drugs

The Act also funds clinical research "for the development and evaluation of new treatments for postpartum conditions, including new biological agents." That means synthetic drugs. The pharmaceutical industry has ensured more tax dollars will continue to flow into its coffers.

"The suicide rate is 718 for every 100,000 people taking SSRI/SNRI drugs in clinical trials," Dr. Arif Khan told NIH [the National Institutes of Health] in August 2002. SSRI/SNRI drugs are antidepressant drugs, which is an oxymoron because the drugs cause depression. They should be called pro-depression drugs. The suicide rate in the general population, not taking psychiatric drugs, is about 11 for every 100,000 people. In fact, all 33 brands of SSRI/SNRI drugs carry the FDA's [US Food and Drug Administration] most severe warning, a Black Box Warning, for suicide. Besides suicide the drugs have more than 100 other severe side effects, including anxiety, panic attacks, irritability, hallucinations, hostility, aggressiveness, and mania. Antidepressants are mind-altering drugs that have never been shown in any clinical study to help depressed people much more than the herb St. John's Wort or the placebo (sugar pill). In one study the placebo group had significantly better results than the group receiving the antidepressant drug, confirming that the body has natural ways to deal with the ups and downs of life.

Its About Money, Not Health

Once people are labeled with a mental disorder, such as postpartum psychosis, their behavior is then blamed on the disorder when in fact the drugs are causing the behavior.

Antidepressants' Adverse Impacts on Mom and Baby

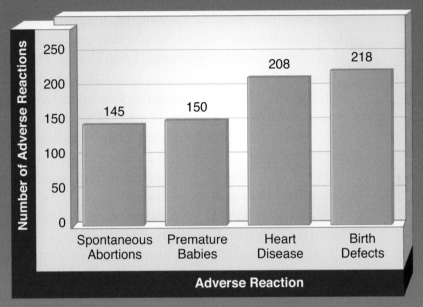

Adverse drug reactions reported to the US Food and Drug Administration's MedWatch reporting system concerning pregnant women taking SSRI antidepressants from 2004–2007

Taken from: Uniteforlife.org, "The Bitter Pill: Reasons Why The Mothers Act Must Not Be Passed." 2009.

For a real life example, check out Amy Philo's story on You Tube. She was anxious because her newborn son had a severe allergic reaction to a formula given to her by a physician. Amy's fear and anxiety for her child was absolutely normal and would have subsided once she had her baby safely at home. Instead, she was diagnosed as suffering from postpartum depression and given an antidepressant. She asked if the drug would be safe for her baby since she was breast-feeding. A physician told her yes, the drug would make her baby happy too. Research results do not support what the doctor told Amy. "In conclusion, our results suggest that maternal exposure to fluoxetine (Prozac, Luvox, Sarafem, and Symbyax) during pregnancy and lactation results in enduring behavioral alterations throughout life." All psychiatric drugs, including antidepressants, are neurotoxins. That means they kill nerve cells everywhere in the body.

"[Amy says,] After only being on the antidepressant for a couple of days I had thoughts of killing my baby." Amy was horrified, but instead of blaming the drug's known side effects, the physician blamed the label of postpartum depression. Obviously, Amy's "mental illness" had worsened and she now needed to be put in a psychiatric ward. She didn't agree to the incarceration but her resistance was again labeled as due to her mental illness. The white coats know best! Fortunately Amy's story has a happy ending. She suspected the antidepressant was causing her strange thought patterns. She managed to be released from the psychiatric ward after only a brief stay and she stopped taking the drugs they had given her. All of Amy's symptoms that had been labeled by the medical community as postpartum depression symptoms ceased when she stopped taking the drugs. Her baby and she were home together; a happy ending. That will not be the case when they initiate the Mothers Act. Since every mother is potential income to psychiatry and the pharmaceutical industry, we can predict that the majority of new mothers will be labeled and drugged for postpartum depression. It is about money, not health.

The pharmaceutical industry and psychiatry are conjoined twins joined at the wallet. "Adoption of the Mothers Act is a positive development for women and their families," says Alan F. Schatzberg, MD, President of the American Psychiatric Association (APA). Schatzberg was one of several influential psychiatrists who Senator Grassley's investigations found had failed to disclose financial ties to pharmaceutical companies.

"In order to survive we psychiatrists must go where the money is," Dr. Steven Sharfstein, APA Vice President told Congress. The money is in prescription psychiatric drugs as demonstrated by the astounding fact that in 2007 the five leading psychiatric drugs grossed more money than the gross national product of half the countries in the world.

Believing Absurdities

The French philosopher Voltaire wrote, "Those who can make you believe absurdities, can make you commit atrocities." The conjoined twins of the pharmaceutical industry and psychiatry are doing their best to have the public believe the absurdity that the stress and emotional roller coaster of becoming a new mother is a mental illness. Then they get these vulnerable women to commit the atrocity of taking mind-altering, addictive antidepressant drugs that go directly into the baby through the mother's milk. These drugs can make a new mother's life a living hell. Ask Amy Philo.

Even if the mother does not suffer visible side effects from an antidepressant, she is still consuming an addictive drug that is a neurotoxin. And if she breast feeds, her baby is consuming a drug that has been shown to cause severe, irreparable damage.

Pregnant women taking antidepressants have babies who are 6 times more likely to have primary pulmonary hypertension (PPH) or a developing lung disorder. PPH is extremely serious. The drug causes developmental distortion of the lungs leading to lack of oxygen to crucial organs such as the brain, kidneys and liver. PPH is often fatal. Babies who initially survive PPH have long-term health problems including breathing difficulties, seizures and developmental disorders.

The Mothers Act will encourage all new mothers to submit to mental health screening for a psychiatric disorder that was voted into existence. It will not get to the root cause of a woman's temporary depression after giving birth.

Treatment for Postpartum Depression Is More Important than Breast-Feeding

Lisa Sniderman

In the following viewpoint Lisa Sniderman asserts that some women with postpartum depression should stay on their medications even if it means they have to give up breast-feeding. According to Sniderman, women whose untreated depression leaves them unable to emotionally respond to their children are better off staying on their medications and bonding with their children in ways other than breast-feeding. Sniderman says she used to feel guilty about not breast-feeding. However, she has learned to let go of the guilt and says that staying on medications or going off of them to breast-feed is a personal decision each woman must decide for herself. Lisa Sniderman's essay was posted on Katherine Stone's blog *Postpartum Progress*, which provides information for pregnant women and new mothers about mental illnesses associated with childbirth.

I'm a PPD [postpartum depression] survivor who braved it and had another kid. Along the way, I even survived two years of fertility treatment and three miscarriages. And guess what? NO depression this time around. I am deliriously in love with my kids and my life. Turns out newborns are enchanting. Who knew? The first time around, I was too consumed with depression and guilt to notice. Now my stomach does giddy flip-flops whenever I cuddle my son. I could do without the sleep deprivation and 20 extra pounds, and I wish a trip to Costco didn't take all day, but I'm able to take these things in stride. That amazes me.

Staying on Medications Helped Me to Become a Better Mother

I don't attribute this outcome to dumb luck. We went into pregnancy #2 with a solid plan. I stayed on my full dose of antidepressant throughout the pregnancy, and started on a mood stabilizer immediately after giving birth. As a result, I bottle-fed my son from the beginning and never looked back. I made this decision peacefully before I even got pregnant this time, even though I strongly support breastfeeding in general. I did my best over the years to find other treatment options, and they just didn't work for me. As I watched my first baby become a toddler, then a highly verbal preschooler, I discovered that it is a mother's guilt—far more than her chosen feeding method—which presents the true barrier to emotional bonding. Once I resolved that guilt, I began to mother my child from my heart, if not from my breasts. It would have been nice not to have to choose between the two, but I made the right choice.

> **FAST FACT**
>
> A twenty-year-long study published in the American Journal of Psychiatry in 2006 found that children with depressed parents suffered about triple the rate of anxiety disorders and depression by their thirties, were in poorer health, and were much more likely to be dependent on drugs and alcohol than children whose parents had no mental disorders.

In fact, I'd venture to say that getting effective treatment for serious mental illness is *always* the right choice. For the baby as well as the mom.

Four years ago I was locked into a recursive loop of self-hate that left me unable to respond to my baby. Medication and therapy helped unlock the loop and reclaim my maternal wisdom and instincts. Getting my own needs met has enabled me to gladly and willingly make sacrifices for my children, instead of experiencing those sacrifices as misery and depletion. For example, in January I used up all my vacation time to help my daughter with a potty-training "immersion" program for kids with bowel conditions. We stayed at home and practiced over and over again for three weeks. Some days we both fell asleep after dinner, totally exhausted, and started again at dawn. I never once yelled or showed impatience—I provided the supportive presence she needed to work through the challenge. When she finally got the hang of it, I was so proud of us both that I cried. My therapist remarked, "This was your version of the breast-feeding experience." She was right!

When dealing with postpartum depression, women may have to choose between breast-feeding or taking medications that would require them to bottle-feed their babies. (© Catchlight Visual Services/ Alamy.)

Breast-Feeding and Psychiatric Medications

Medication	American Academy of Pediatrics Rating
SSRI and TCA	Effects unknown but may be of concern
Benzodiazepine	Effects unknown but may be of concern
Lithium	Use with caution
Carbamazepine and VPA	Compatible with breast-feeding
Lamotrigine	Effects unknown but may be of concern
Typical antipsychotics (most)	Effects unknown but may be of concern
Clozapine	Effects unknown but may be of concern
Other atypical antipsychotics	Not Rated

Taken from: Madeline Becker, Geraldine Mayor, and Elizabeth Kunkel. "Psychotropic Medications and Breastfeeding." *Primary Psychiatry*, 2009.

It really bugs me that our culture tends to view a mother's self-care and mental health as some sort of luxury, when in fact true selflessness cannot occur in their absence. You have to possess a whole self in order to set it aside. In the throes of PPD, struggling to make a decision about my meds, I thought comments such as, "A happy mom means a happy baby," and, "You have to put on your own oxygen mask first" were just well-intentioned platitudes. Four years later, I see how profound these statements really are. My daughter doesn't stay up nights wondering why she wasn't breastfed, but she sure notices when I am emotionally unavailable. My infant son can already tell the difference between a forced smile and a genuine one, between a feeding that is rushed and one that is attuned. Kids are amazingly perceptive that way. They learn how to regard themselves and their world by watching our faces and witnessing our actions. What we say doesn't matter much if we're hypocrites about it.

I still do feel sad at the loss of the breastfeeding relationship. But sadness is different than guilt. It's a productive emotion that can be worked through. It doesn't paralyze me. While I support a pro-breastfeeding culture, I don't see anything positive about creating guilt in women who fail at breastfeeding, for whatever reason. This guilt is unproductive, and can be very disabling. I know that breastfeeding—when it works out—is an incomparable gift to both mom and baby, something that is worth a lot of sacrifice and time. However, a mother's mental health is not an acceptable sacrifice, and that's where a lot of depressed women get confused and stuck. It's not hard to understand why.

Parent-Child Attachment Happens in Many Ways

In our society, "breast versus bottle" can be shorthand for "mother versus mother." Breastfeeding has become an issue of individual morality, not just a policy and public-health concern, and I think that's a mistake. Total strangers malign each other's character, both in the media and in real life. No matter what a mother does, she can be sure someone will disapprove. Added to this, of course, is all the stigma and misunderstanding that surround post-partum mental illness. The fallout from this combined storm is the private suffering of individual mothers. If you are suffering with postpartum mental illness, I hope my words give you the courage to make the best treatment decision for yourself, whether or not it involves exclusive breastfeeding. Each mother is the expert on her own subjective experience, and she is the one who has to live it. Once I recognized this truth for myself, I stopped caring so much what other people think.

I know in my gut that my kids are lucky to have me as their mom. At its core, parent-child attachment is based on the parent's responsiveness to the child's needs, respect for their unique personhood, and ability to assume their point of view. Because my mothering has these qualities, I consider myself an attachment parent even though I bottle-feed.

(Heck, I still use a sling and cloth diapers, because for me it isn't all-or-nothing. I do what I can, and I don't do what I can't.) I am in love with being a mother. For me, that begins and ends with taking care of my mental health. Oops, I hear my son beginning to cry, so I'm going to hold him close as I feed him a bottle. What a wonderful experience for us both!

Breast-Feeding Can Help Lessen Postpartum Depression

Kathleen A. Kendall-Tackett

In the following viewpoint Kathleen Kendall-Tackett maintains that breast-feeding is beneficial for depressed moms, and it should be encouraged, not discouraged. According to Kendall-Tackett, research shows that depression rates are lower in moms who breast-feed compared to moms who do not. Studies also show, says Kendall-Tackett, that breast-feeding protects infants from the negative effects of their mother's depression. Kendall-Tackett asserts that depressed moms should not have to decide between their mental health and breast-feeding. She says doctors should accommodate women with post-partum depression and help them find breast-feeding-friendly treatment methods. Kendall-Tackett is a health psychologist, an International Board Certified Lactation Consultant, and a clinical associate professor of pediatrics at Texas Tech University School of Medicine. She is the author or editor of many books in the fields of trauma, women's health, depression, and breast-feeding, including the 2005 book *Depression in New Mothers*.

SOURCE: Kathleen A. Kendall-Tackett, "Breastfeeding Beats the Blues," *Mothering*, September/October 2010, pp. 60, 62–66, 68. Copyright © 2010 by Mothering Magazine. All rights reserved. Reproduced by permission.

Each year, hundreds of thousands of women who have given birth—about 10 to 20 percent of new mothers—will become depressed. Depression affects how women feel about themselves, their partners, and even their babies. The consequences are so serious that health organizations, such as the American College of Obstetrics and Gynecology, have launched major initiatives to identify and treat depression in new mothers.

Permission to Wean

Over the past 16 years, as a health psychologist, La Leche League leader, and lactation consultant, I've spoken with thousands of women with postpartum depression (PPD). While the details of their stories have differed, two aspects have always been the same: They have been diagnosed with depression and told to wean their children. "Motherhood is not about martyrdom," their doctors told them. "We're giving you *permission* to wean. Your mental health is more important than the supposed benefits of breastfeeding. Besides, formula is just as good.

But the mothers who called me didn't see it that way. For them, breastfeeding was much more than the mere delivery of a superior infant-feeding product. They spoke of the emotional attachment and connection they felt when their babies were at the breast, and of the tremendous sense of loss they experienced when they were told to give up what they felt was the only thing that was going well for them. In short, new mothers with depression faced an awful choice: care for their own mental health or care for their babies. It's a choice no woman should ever have to make.

I made it my mission to educate health-care providers about treatments for depression that are breastfeeding-friendly. It seemed a significant leap forward when the PPD community finally—*finally*—was willing to accommodate breastfeeding mothers. But recently, the discourse

Studies have shown that breast-feeding may reduce post-partum depression, due to the emotional bond created between a mother and her infant during nursing. (Picture Partners/Photo Researchers, Inc.)

has shifted. Breastfeeding is tolerated, but many of the behaviors that support it, such as breastfeeding at night, breastfeeding on cue, and bed sharing, are frowned on. Indeed, mothers are sometimes actively encouraged to disconnect from their babies as a way to lower their risk for depression. For example, mothers are advised to skip nighttime feedings, as described in the popular book *Postpartum Depression for Dummies*.

Even for moms with fresh buns out of the oven, sleeping is not a luxury—it's a medical necessity! . . . Humans need 8.4 hours of *uninterrupted* sleep per night in order to function at their best (the key word here being *uninterrupted*). . . . Sleep in a separate area away from the baby and the adult on duty. Use earplugs and a white noise machine . . . if necessary. The goal is to make sure that you aren't hearing the baby or other noises so you can achieve uninterrupted sleep. . . . If you're breastfeeding or pumping, it's important to empty both breasts before bed so you won't be awakened engorged and in pain during your off-duty shift. If you can pump during the day, your partner can use your milk for the off-duty feedings.

A variant of this advice, for professionals, is offered in this description of a program designed to prevent postpartum depression:

[T]he Women's Health Concerns Clinic at St. Joseph's Healthcare has developed a preventive intervention that is routinely offered to patients who present with high risk for postpartum depression (e.g., those with personal or family history of depression, those with subclinical symptoms of depression during pregnancy). These patients are offered a hospital stay of up to 5 days, a private hospital room and rooming-out of the infant at night. Women who choose to breast-feed are encouraged to pump milk during the day for nighttime feedings, use formula for night feedings or ask to be woken only when necessary to feed. Benzodiazepines are prescribed if required to encourage consistent nighttime sleep onset for the first postpartum week.

If avoiding nighttime feedings isn't enough to avert depression, mothers are simply told to wean. Unfortunately, this advice fails to recognize the importance of breastfeeding to the mother—not only as a way to feed her baby, but as a way to help her cope with depression. In her account of her own experience of PPD, actress Brooke Shields describes how she was pressured to wean, but felt that breastfeeding was the only thing keeping her sane: "If I were to eliminate [breast-feeding], I might have no hope of coming through this nightmare. I was hanging on to the breast-feeding as my lifeline."

Women's Stories of How Breastfeeding Helped

Another mother who contacted me described how breastfeeding helped her overcome an anxiety disorder and panic attacks following the birth of her baby. She, too, had been advised to wean in order to make things easier for her:

> When my first was born, I was completely overwhelmed with the feeling of being her primary caregiver. I had no family or friends in the area, and my husband had to go back to work when she was five or six days old. I had panic attacks, and felt like there was no way I was up to being the kind of parent she deserved. Breastfeeding was going well, though, and it was often the only thing that I felt like I was doing right. . . .

> Well-meaning family and friends often tried to suggest that I let my husband give her a bottle, to reduce the "burden" on me of caring for her. They also suggested that if we moved her out of our bed, I could get more and better sleep, and recover more easily. I knew that keeping her close at night helped to make it more OK that I wasn't holding her all the time during the day, and also that I was able to get more sleep and rest by nursing her in bed. As things started to improve for me hormonally, I was able to look back at the fact that I met her most basic needs, even as I was struggling, and it helped me feel better about myself, which helped my emotional healing. I know that the advice I received came with good intentions, but I was so vulnerable then, and I wanted a magic cure to all of my problems.

I seriously considered sleep training, and letting my husband give her an occasional bottle of formula, even though it didn't feel right. I am to glad that my husband was strong enough to help me through that horrible time in other ways, and always remind me of our daughter's needs in a kind and loving way.

As difficult as it is for mothers whose breastfeeding experiences are going well, it's far worse for mothers who struggle with *both* depression and breastfeeding problems, which only intensify the pressure to wean—as the next mother describes. Her new daughter at first had difficulty latching on, which resulted in her gaining weight at a rate lower than the average.

> I never bonded with Annabel. Those first few weeks were hell, because we were struggling with breastfeeding, struggling to get her weight back up to the arbitrary percentage they require, and our families were . . . less than helpful. When she was six days old, my mother, father, and sister sat downstairs and discussed how awful it was that I was persisting on this breastfeeding crap, how they couldn't believe we let her sleep in our bed, and that I probably hadn't had a shower since I had her. . . . The only thing they did to help while they were here was hold her and order takeout. The takeout was helpful. The same was true for most of our family visitors and sadly, most of our friends. One of my friends folded laundry while I nursed Annabel. I cried uncontrollably, because it was the first nice thing I felt someone did for me besides bringing me food and cooing over the baby.

New Research About Depression and Breastfeeding

As the above stories illustrate, it's common for women to be told to wean if they show any signs of depression, or even of stress. This advice is unfortunate, and in many

Depressed Moms Less Likely to Breast-Feed

Depressed Moms

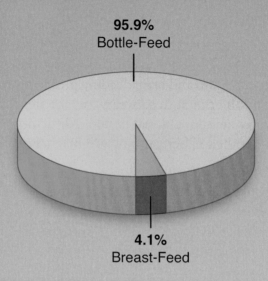

95.9%
Bottle-Feed

4.1%
Breast-Feed

Not Depressed Moms

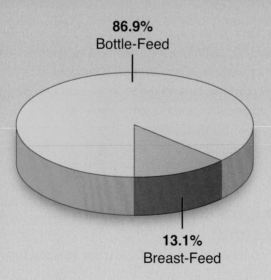

86.9%
Bottle-Feed

13.1%
Breast-Feed

Taken from: E. Sibolboro Mezzacappa and J. Endicott. "Parity Mediates the Association Between Infant Feeding Method and Maternal Depressive Symptoms." *Archives of Women's Mental Health*, 2007.

cases just plain wrong. It also runs counter to a growing number of studies that indicate that breastfeeding actually protects women's mental health.

A recent review of 49 studies found that rates of depression are lower in breastfeeding mothers than in their non-breastfeeding counterparts, and that *formula feeding* is a risk factor for depression. Breastfeeding protects women's mental health because it lowers stress. For example, a study of 43 breastfeeding women found that breastfeeding significantly decreased women's levels of stress hormones. Further, hormones related to breastfeeding, such as oxytocin and prolactin, have both anti-depressant and anti-anxiety effects.

This is not to say that breastfeeding mothers never get depressed—for they certainly do. But breastfeeding lowers women's risk of depression, and can aid in their recovery from it. Breastfeeding also protects babies while their mothers are depressed. Many studies have demonstrated the negative effects of mothers' depression on the development of infants and children. One study, however, tried to determine whether breastfeeding protected babies from the negative effects of depression—and found that it did: Breastfeeding protected babies because depressed, breastfeeding mothers touched, stroked, and made eye contact with their babies more than did depressed, non-breastfeeding women. These behaviors are built into the breastfeeding relationship. Non-breastfeeding, depressed women are more likely to disengage from their babies and less likely to respond to their cues. Such disengagement leads to many of the negative effects of maternal depression.

What New Research Says About Breastfeeding and Sleep

Infant sleep is another area in which depressed mothers are vulnerable to unsolicited—and/or often wrong—advice. To decrease their risk for PPD, mothers are often told to avoid nighttime breastfeeding. We know that if mothers follow this advice, it will likely have a negative impact on breastfeeding. The most immediate effect will likely be on a mother's milk supply. Skipping nighttime breastfeeding in those early weeks can be enough to permanently lower her supply—at least for this specific baby, which can lead to early weaning. And when that occurs, there are long-term effects for both mother and baby. But let's put that issue aside for the moment and consider whether avoiding nighttime breastfeeding actually does preserve women's mental health. In short, is this good advice?

At first glance, it may seem to be. Since breastmilk is lower in fat and protein than formula, we might assume that breastfeeding mothers sleep less than their formula-feeding counterparts. The idea behind this line of reasoning is that formula's higher concentrations of fat and protein may sustain babies for longer, possibly increasing the amount of time that they—and, in turn, their mothers—sleep. When a mother's mental health is at stake, avoiding nighttime breastfeeding might be worth the risk it poses to the milk supply and the mother's ability to exclusively breastfeed. However, recent research has revealed the opposite to be true: namely, that exclusively breastfeeding mothers actually get more and better-quality sleep than mothers who are exclusively formula feeding or supplementing with formula. And that has major implications for the mothers' mental health.

For example, a study of 33 mothers at four weeks postpartum found that bedsharing, breastfeeding mothers got more sleep than mothers who were bottle-feeding. In another study, the sleep of the parents of exclusively breastfed infants was compared with the sleep of the parents of infants who were supplemented with formula or were exclusively fed formula. Mothers who exclusively breastfed slept an average of 40 minutes more than mothers who supplemented.

Most recent is a study of 2,830 women at seven weeks postpartum. The researchers found that disrupted sleep was a major risk factor for postpartum depression. But here is where it gets really interesting: *Mothers who were not exclusively breastfeeding had more disrupted sleep and a higher risk of depression.*

Not only do breastfeeding mothers get more sleep, the sleep they get is of better quality. Another study compared 22 exclusively breastfeeding women, 12 age-matched control women, and 7 women who were exclusively bottle-feeding. The breastfeeding mothers got an average of 182 minutes of slow-wave sleep (SWS) per night, while women in the control group had an average of 86 minutes, and the exclusively bottle-feeding women had an average of 63 minutes. Slow-wave sleep is an important marker of sleep quality; a low percentage of SWS is associated with daytime fatigue and depression.

The results of these studies are remarkably consistent: Breastfeeding mothers are less tired and get more sleep than their formula- or mixed-feeding counterparts, and this difference in sleep *lowers* their risk for depression. As one study noted,

> Using supplementation as a coping strategy for minimizing sleep loss can actually be detrimental because of its effect on prolactin hormone production and secretion. . . . Maintenance of breast-feeding as well as deep restorative sleep stages may be greatly compromised for new mothers who cope with infant feedings by supplementing in an effort to get more sleep time.

In sum, advising women to avoid nighttime breastfeeding to lessen their risk of depression is not medically sound. In fact, if women follow this advice, it may actually *increase* their risk of depression.

> **FAST FACT**
>
> According to an analysis of data from the US National Maternal and Infant Health Survey, the rate of depression for first-time mothers who breast-feed is higher than the rate of depression for breast-feeding mothers who have already had one or more children.

The Road to Recovery: How Attachment Parenting Can Help

Perhaps the most important conclusion from all of this recent research is that breastfeeding and keeping mothers and babies together is good for women's mental health. Indeed, separating mothers and babies will likely prove counterproductive. Babies and mothers alike are more stressed when they are apart. With breastfeeding, nature has built in a lovely way for mothers to counter the stressors of new motherhood. And attachment parenting supports breastfeeding and also protects mothers' mental health.

Attachment parenting also helps mothers feel that they are doing a good job as mothers, even when they're struggling with depression. This mother describes how her son's reflux and his difficulties in breastfeeding affected her mental state and how she felt as a parent:

> I think attachment parenting was really critical to my reconnection to my baby. . . . I was really struck by how others, even those who were experts in the field, were discouraging of cosleeping, wanted me to have others bottle-feed him, and generally thought that "a break from the baby" was what I needed. What I really needed (and what I often advocate for in my role as a supporter of other moms) was support so that I could cope better with being with and caring for my unhappy baby. Here's how attachment parenting impacted us:

> Cosleeping—This was the only way to get him back to the breast, which was critical to both his well-being and mine. . . . It also meant that I got more sleep, and I wasn't worried about his well-being, because I could locate him easily and check on him.

> Babywearing—I think this was the most critical piece for us. First of all, he'd sleep (finally!) in a sling, snuggled in an upright position. This made me happy, and also kept us in close proximity. He's getting big now (14 months

old), and I haven't switched him to a backpack yet. . . . Having his warm body against mine kept the good hormones flowing.

Cue reading—I really believe that reading cues is integral to my parenting style. . . . What was so hard about our situation was the feeling that, as he got sicker, his cues made no sense to me. I'm not sure if it was his pain speaking, or my anxiety clouding my thinking, or both. . . . Being able to read his cues made me feel as if I was finally a parent again.

Listening to Mothers

The mothers I have spoken with acknowledge that people are trying to be helpful by giving them "permission" to wean or get away from their babies. There can be times when this is the best course, but we should not assume that it always is. This is not what the women who shared their stories with me felt they needed. What they wanted instead was support for their parenting decisions, including breastfeeding:

What makes me angry is that no one supported me in my desire to breastfeed, I was undermined at every turn, by doctors, nurses, even a lactation consultant. . . . It took me three weeks for someone besides my super husband to tell me I was doing a good thing for my baby and a good thing for myself. I was told I just needed sleep, or that I held her too much, or that she wasn't getting enough milk. All I had were people undermining my attempt to breastfeed, all to try and spare me "guilt": "Oh, formula is just fine. It isn't rat poison. Your baby will he happy and healthy, and that's what matters."

Well, what about me? What about what I want, and what I want to give my baby? When does what *Mom* wants come into the picture, rather than what everyone else thinks Mom wants or feels? I have never felt more devalued, more undermined, or less of a person than I did when I had psychosis. Everyone spoke loud and clear, and what they said was, "You can't be a good mom if you breastfeed. You are not a good mom now because you are breastfeeding." Well, they were all wrong. I was sick and I needed help. I needed someone to tell me that, by God, I was a good mom, and that I was doing the best for my baby. I needed someone to offer to do my laundry. I needed someone to clean my kitchen, or go to the grocery store. I didn't need any more nonsense about how I would feel better if I just weaned, or if I put the baby on a schedule, or any other crap like that.

This mother was so depressed that she had made detailed suicide plans, a particularly ominous sign. The only thing that stopped her was the fact that she was breastfeeding:

I needed support, and I didn't get it until it was almost too late.

If I had weaned, I would have committed suicide. That day, I know this for a fact. The one time I was frustrated and went to mix a bottle of formula, I stopped. I knew if I mixed that formula, I would feed it to her, and walk directly to the garage [where she planned to kill herself]. I never mixed a bottle of formula, because as much as I wanted to die, I wanted to give my baby the best. I was a good mom in the midst of the fog, but no one else would see it.

You read my thoughts of protecting women from guilt over breastfeeding. People tried to do that to me. If they had been successful, I'd be dead. I wish people would stop assuming that women need protecting.

With help and support, women can overcome depression, and in order to help, we must first listen to them. But when we *assume* that we know what women need, we disempower the very mothers we seek to help, and we present them with a false choice: their mental health vs. caring for their babies. The good news is that, with proper care and support, they can have both—as this mother describes:

> Depression runs in my family. . . . I don't know why I am insulated from [it], but I wonder if finding attachment parenting as the most natural parenting strategy for me/us helped. . . . Is it because of AP? I don't know, but I know attachment parenting makes me a better person . . . a more confident parent. I think it helps.

Postpartum Depression Should Be a Legal Defense for Women Who Kill Their Children

John Floyd and Billy Sinclair

In the following viewpoint John Floyd and Billy Sinclair argue that postpartum depression, postpartum psychosis, and other postpartum mental disorders should be a legal defense for women who murder their children. Floyd and Sinclair discuss cases of infanticide in Texas and say that the women involved were suffering from a postpartum mental disorder and were in "demented states." The public needs to be educated about postpartum mental disorders say Floyd and Sinclair. Women who murder their children need help not punishment, they say. Floyd is a criminal defense attorney and Sinclair is a paralegal. They work in Houston, Texas.

The postpartum depression debate has awakened once again in Harris County [Texas] in the case of Narjes Modarresi, who is accused of killing her two-month-old son. Anytime a mother harms her child

SOURCE: John Floyd and Billy Sinclair, "The Tragedy of Postpartum Depression, Psychosis, and Infanticide," *Criminal Jurisdiction*, May 1, 2010. www.JohnTFloyd.com. Copyright © 2010 by John Floyd. Reproduced by permission.

deep-seated emotions are stirred in the community. Mothers are protective by nature. It's an instinct rooted in the DNA of all animals, especially humans.

Modarresi's attorney, George Parnham, recently [April 26, 2010] informed the local media that his client was walking around "zombie-like" in the days preceding the death of little Masih Golabbakhsh.

"After the birth of the first child, she was treated at Ben Taub (General Hospital) for 36 days," Parnham said. "By all family accounts, after the birth of the second child, she was zombie-like for two months."

A Defense for Women Who Kill Their Children

Parnham said he is still trying to gather and assess all the facts before deciding whether to present an insanity defense as he successfully did in the Andrea Yates case—a Clear Lake [Texas] mother who drowned her five children in a bathtub in 2001. Yates was found not guilty by reason of insanity at her second trial in 2006 and committed to a state mental hospital.

Just last year Rep. Jessica Farrar, . . . introduced a bill in the Texas Legislature that would have made postpartum mental disorder a legal defense for women who kill their children within 12 months of giving birth. The *Dallas Morning News* reported that the bill, had it passed, would have made Texas "the first state to have an infanticide law."

"It's something every civilized country has on its books," Parnham, a staunch supporter of the bill, told the *Morning News*. "The only thing that will change public attitude is education about postpartum issues."

Parnham and Rep. Farrar are members of *Postpartum Support International* ("PSI") founded in 1987 by Jane Honikman and headquartered in Santa Barbara, California. The purpose of the organization "is to increase awareness among public and professional communities about the emotional changes that women experience during pregnancy and postpartum."

PSI reports that 15% of all women will experience postpartum depression following the birth of a child while 10% will suffer some form of depression or anxiety during pregnancy itself. This mental health issue affects the entire family as it has the Golabbakhsh family. This was made clear in a recent *Houston Chronicle* report about the case: "... the baby's father, Amir Golabbakhsh, and his relatives, stood silently behind Parnham as he addressed the media," wrote *Chronicle* reporter Cindy George. "At times, they hung their heads and the child's grandmother, Doris Golabbakhsh, gripped a folded handkerchief. The only person who spoke, one of the child's uncles, stepped to the podium to simply give the correct pronunciation of Modarresi's name."

The volatile debate about whether postpartum depression is a legitimate legal defense for murder was reignited during the trial of Narjes Modarresi (center), who was accused of killing her two-month-old son in Harris County, Texas. (© AP Images/Houston Chronicle, James Nielsen.)

Help, Not Punishment

It is the damage postpartum-related crimes causes the families of the victim as well as the mother that prompted Andrea Yates' former husband, Russell Yates, to speak out about the issue, urging the community to keep an "open mind" about this mental health issue. "The awareness of postpartum illness has improved," Russell Yates told Cindy George. "I don't think it's such a taboo. I think Andrea's case helped to raise awareness of postpartum illness, and I think on the whole we have a better understanding. . . . It's hard to blame someone for becoming ill."

We agree. Narjes Modarresi is a living tragedy. Her life, and the lives of her family, will never be the same again. No matter what happens to Narjes, her family has been sentenced to a life term of second-guessing, grappling with the unknown of a mental illness about which very little is still known.

In most crimes, there is someone to point a finger of blame at. We can collectively feel good seeing them brought to account and made to pay for their wrongdoing. But as Russell Yates asked: how do you blame, much less punish, someone for being ill? By all accounts Narjes Modarresi is a good human being. She simply could not endure the rigors of pregnancy and fulfill the responsibilities of motherhood because she suffers from a terrible mental disorder.

> **FAST FACT**
>
> According to legal scholars, at least twenty-nine countries, not including the United States, have laws that assign more lenient penalties in cases of infanticide by a woman with a mental illness.

Insanity Based on Postpartum Disorder Is Difficult to Prove

Under Texas Penal Code 19.01(a), prosecutors will have to prove that Narjes intentionally, knowingly, recklessly, or with criminal negligence caused the death of her son. Section 8.01(a) of the Penal Code offers Narjes an "affirmative defense" of showing that at the time she killed her

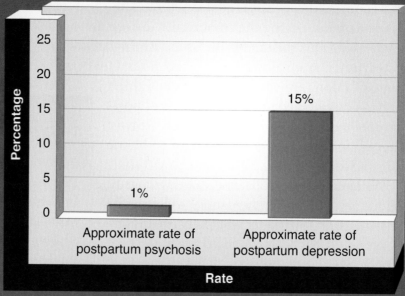

Postpartum Psychosis Is Rare

Percentage

25
20
15
10
5
0

15%

1%

Approximate rate of
postpartum psychosis

Approximate rate of
postpartum depression

Rate

Taken from: www.postpartum.net.

son, her conduct was the "result of severe mental disease or defect" which deprived her of the ability to know her conduct was wrong.

An insanity defense based on a postpartum disorder is difficult to establish as Columbia University's Associate Professor of Psychiatry Margaret Spinelli, an expert on mental illness and infanticide, told the *Morning News:* "The insanity defense can be an extremely strict law as it is in Texas and other states. People have to fit a very specific criteria to meet it."

The difficulty in the insanity defense was seen during several fairly recent Texas infanticide cases. Besides the Andrea Yates case, *Chronicle* columnist Rick Casey recently wrote about three other cases: Lisa Diaz, Deanna Laney, and Dena Schlosser. Diaz, a Plano mother of two

PERSPECTIVES ON DISEASES AND DISORDERS

children, killed the 3 and 5 year olds before stabbing herself. She said she thought she was saving the children from evil spirits. Laney of Tyler killed two of her sons by stoning them to death while maiming a third. She also had a religious motive: God ordered her to do it to test her faith. Schlosser, also of Plano, killed her 10-month-old son because, as she told her husband the night before, she wanted to "give her child to God."

Casey pointed out that the psychiatrist, Dr. Park Dietz, hired by prosecutors in both the Yates and Laney cases found Yates to be legally sane while [finding] Laney to be legally insane. As with most people, Casey found the distinction "crazy." He added that "both these women, and apparently at least one of the others, did unspeakable things because in their demented states they thought they were beyond redemption and were afraid their children would become so.

"They were tormented in doing it and would be further tormented when they fully understood what they had done."

Lack of Public Understanding

That's why the general community doesn't truly understand the postpartum issue. This lack of understanding makes the insanity defense so difficult in such cases because the disorder is so rare. Experts like Susan Dowd Stone, chair of PSI, say that less than 1 in a thousand mothers experience "command hallucinations" to kill their children in order to save them. It has not yet been determined if Narjes Modaressi heard any such commands, but attorney Parnham says he plans to hire an Iranian psychiatrist fluent in Farsi to explore this issue. Parnham informed the media that Narjes had expressed concern that her children would "be hurt by a person of negative energy."

This case offers District Attorney [DA] Pat Lykos a chance to address the troubling issue of infanticide brought on by postpartum psychosis. Narjes Modaressi is not a criminal, she is not a murderer. She took the life of her child because she is a deeply troubled person. The criminal justice system is not the appropriate venue in this case to resolve the interests of society, the child's family and Narjes herself. This is an issue where a mother needs treatment, not punishment. The demons in her head which apparently forced her to commit the unspeakable act against her child have punished her enough. Our court system should now find a way to treat her psychosis. The first step in that direction begins with DA Lykos. We hope she will take it.

Postpartum Depression Is Not Always a Valid Legal Defense for Women Who Kill Their Children

Richard E. Vatz

In the following viewpoint Richard E. Vatz contends that women like Andrea Yates who murder their children should be punished and incarcerated. Vatz discusses the case of Andrea Yates, who drowned her five young children in the bathtub of her Texas home in 2001. Yates was found guilty of murder in 2002, but the verdict was later overturned by an appeals court. She was retried in 2006 and this time was found not guilty by reason of insanity. Since then she has been treated in a Texas psychiatric hospital. Vatz believes the first verdict was correct; Yates knew what she was doing and knew it was wrong. Having postpartum depression, says Vatz, does not relieve a person from being responsible for her actions. Vatz is an associate psychology editor at *USA Today* and a professor of rhetoric and communication at Towson University in Maryland.

SOURCE: Richard E. Vatz, "Will Justice Be Served on Andrea Yates?," *USA Today* (Magazine), March 2005. www.usatoday.com. Copyright © 2005 by Society for the Advancement of Education. All rights reserved. Reproduced by permission.

The Texas State Appeals Court's throwing out of Andrea Yates' convictions after drowning her five children should not affect the ultimate disposition of her case. Yates should be incarcerated for the rest of her life. The evidence that she knew exactly what she was doing, notwithstanding the stress she was under, is overwhelming and seemingly without serious contradiction, save for the incredulity of the public.

The cause of the reversible error in the case is the testimony of the generally responsible Park Dietz, the lone psychiatrist for the prosecution. His well-known opposition to the insanity pleas of murderers John Hinckley, Jeffrey Dahmer, and "Unabomber" Theodore Kaczynski laid the groundwork for his testimony for the prosecution. He testified that "shortly before" the Yates drownings, there was a segment of the show *Law and Order* (for which he was a consultant) which dealt with a "woman with postpartum depression who drowned her children in the bathtub and was found insane. . . ."

Pursuant to Dietz's claim, the prosecution said in closing arguments that "maybe" there was evidence that Yates saw from that show that "she could drown her children and get away with it." In addition, the prosecution maintained, she told Dietz that therefore "there is a way out" for her. The court now alleges that there had been no airing of any such episode.

One of the prosecutors, Joseph Owmby, says he hopes to make the appeals panel reconsider. If it does not, Owmby vows to take it to Texas' highest court. He argues that Dietz's error was not material. To the contrary: The allegedly false testimony arguably is material in that it well may have substantively affected the verdict. However, it should not have.

To plead insanity successfully in Texas, Yates would have had to prove that she could not tell right from wrong at the time of the killings. The fact that it was she who

called the police is significant evidence that this difficult standard was not satisfied.

Throughout the events of the day of the killings, there was no evidence of Yates' being out of touch with reality or incapable of controlling her actions. Indeed, the opposite is true. These unconscionable acts appeared to be a result of contemptible, but quite rational, decisionmaking. She could not stand her life as it had evolved.

Arriving after her call, Frank Stumpo, a Houston police officer, confronted Yates and recalled asking her, "Do you realize what you have done?" She answered, "Yes, I do; I killed my children." She later stated she was a "bad mother."

Andrea Yates (center) was charged with killing her five children in 2001. Found guilty of murder, her verdict was later overturned by an appeals court. She was later retried and found not guilty by reason of insanity. (© AP Images/Brett Coomer, Pool/FILE.)

Was she out of touch with reality? Did she have premeditation and criminal intent? Undisputed are these facts: She furiously had chased, and eventually killed, the oldest of her children, seven-year-old Noah, who desperately was trying to escape being slaughtered. Moreover, Yates admitted to contemplating murdering her kids for a considerable time before actually doing so. Significantly, evidence of intentional violence in Yates' actions also may have moved the jury, as her hair was found in son John's fist, suggesting he fought against his mother's attack. Imagining the horrible terror Noah must have felt should move any observer to profound sympathy for the victims and equally profound disgust for Yates.

The defense has argued all along that Yates suffered from postpartum depression as well as depression from her father's death prior to the killing of her children. No doubt Yates was depressed. However, depression does not mean that an individual is not responsible for his or her actions. The power of psychiatric rhetoric to mystify is almost impossible to exaggerate. A letter to the editor in the *Baltimore Sun* following the latest court action is prototypical. The author writes, "Ms. Yates was severely depressed and probably schizophrenic as well . . . [the guilty party in the case of the five dead children was] whomever [sic] was responsible for leaving a mentally ill woman in sole charge of five young kids. Ms. Yates was a victim too, and she continues to suffer." The hoary cliché of the perpetrator as victim never seems to die when people are mystified by psychiatrically exculpatory rhetoric.

Depression following childbirth is not unusual—even severe depression, from which psychiatrists estimate that almost half a million women suffer. Still, few children—about 200—are killed each year by their mothers.

In a cover story almost three years ago [July 2, 2001] on the killings, *Newsweek* opined that "Perhaps in some godforsaken way, [Yates] believed that the time had come to set [her children] free." It appears far more accurate to say she felt she had had enough and wanted to end her misery by ending her offspring's lives. The evidence is that Yates became more and more depressed as her parenting obligations increased, leading, for example, to her giving up her job in a cancer clinic.

The problematic testimony given by Dietz may have been a reasonable basis for a new trial. More compelling, the prosecution did communicate incorrectly to the jury that Yates premeditatedly had decided to use a ruse she saw on the nonexistent episode of *Law and Order* to kill

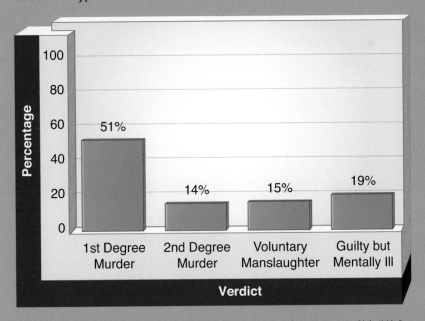

What Verdict Would College Students Give to a Woman Diagnosed with Postpartum Psychosis Who Killed Her Three-Month-Old Baby?

Based on a survey of seventy-five college students taking a class on abnormal psychology who were asked to provide a range of verdicts based on hypothetical cases.

Taken from: Norman J. Finkel, John E. Burke, and Leticia J. Chavez. "Common Sense Judgments of Infanticide." *Psychology, Public Policy, and Law,* 2000.

her kids while claiming insanity as a strategy for escaping punishment.

As to whether there was such an episode continues to be a point at issue. Dietz argues that the *Law and Order* segment "Angel" indeed "premiered in 1995 and aired as recently as five months before the Yates homicides. The character in 'Angel' killed her children, claimed God told her to do it, and entered a plea of insanity. My mistaken recollection was that the plea succeeded in the TV show when, in fact, it failed in fiction as it failed for Mrs. Yates." Perplexingly, the *Law and Order* synopsis of the episode that Dietz claims referenced these issues does not appear to do so. (A synopsis from the program's website notes: "A mother claiming that her baby was kidnapped while she was at confession retraces her steps and actions with Curtis, which raises legal questions later when her attorney introduces a unique defense"), but the court turned the case over for precisely the following reason, articulated in the Texas Court of Appeals opinion: "It is uncontested that the testimony of Dr. Dietz regarding his consultation on a 'Law & Order' television show having a plot remarkably similar to the acts committed by appellant was untrue and that there was no 'Law & Order' television show with such a plot."

Disputed sources of evidentiary facts aside, Andrea Yates should be reprosecuted for murder and, pending the evidence introduced at that trial, she should be reconvicted. Unlike the outcome of a successful insanity defense which would lead to her release when doctors conclude that she no longer is mentally ill, a conviction would keep her imprisoned for life.

At all costs, the country must avoid a release at some future date of Mrs. Yates, for the sake of those who loved—or even for those who have followed the devastating saga of—the murdered Yates children.

Men Can Get Postpartum Depression Too

Emily Anthes

In the following viewpoint Emily Anthes asserts that men can get post-partum depression too. According to Anthes, studies have shown that the stress of bringing a new baby home can affect fathers as much as mothers, and men may even experience hormonal changes after the birth of a child. Still, says Anthes, doctors are sometimes reluctant to say that men are actually experiencing postpartum depression. She says this is unfortunate because, like maternal depression, paternal depression can have detrimental effects on children. Anthes says post-partum depression in dads is a real problem and should be recognized. Emily Anthes is a science and health writer. Her work has appeared in *Scientific American Mind*, *Psychology Today*, *Discover*, and *Slate*.

L ast week [in May 2010], the American Academy of Pediatrics [AAP] officially recommended that pediatricians begin screening their infant patients' mothers for signs of postpartum depression. It's a compelling and simple idea—tired and stressed moms may not take the time to see their own doctors, but you can bet that they won't miss a single appointment with the pediatrician. Now the AAP should go one more step and recommend that the babies' doctors look out for depression in new dads, too.

It Is Not Just Women Who Get PPD

In the last few years, studies have revealed that it's not just women whose moods can plummet after they become parents. In a 2006 study, James Paulson, a psychologist at Eastern Virginia Medical School, assessed the parents of 5,089 infants and found that 14 percent of the mothers had signs of moderate to severe depression. And so did 10 percent of the fathers. Compare that with the 3 percent to 5 percent of men in the general population who are depressed (as well as the 8 percent or 9 percent of women).

Though the percentages vary, other studies have backed up the idea that for men, as well as women, parenthood can cause a bump in the rates of mood disorders. Depression in new fathers has spawned Web sites and support groups, articles by dads struggling with their new roles, and even a storyline in ABC's *Desperate Housewives* [TV show] this fall.

Understudied and Controversial

Still, PPD for dads remains understudied, under-recognized, and controversial. Even among scientists who research the baby blues in new fathers, there's debate about whether "postpartum depression" is the right term. One researcher told me that when talking about men, he prefers "depression during the postnatal period." Whatever you call it, distress after a baby is born is much easier to explain among moms. Pregnancy and childbirth, of course, are hugely taxing and exhausting for women. And, of course, these processes can wreak havoc with a woman's hormones and, thereby, her psychological wellbeing.

Researchers have found that parenthood causes hormonal changes in men, too. The author contends that postpartum depression among fathers remains largely unrecognized and under-researched. (© Bubbles Photolibrary/ Alamy)

Over the last decade, however, researchers have discovered that, lo and behold, parenthood prompts hormonal changes in men, too. (More on that here.) Although the hormonal roller coaster is less pronounced in dads, it could certainly contribute to lousy mood.

What's more, researchers are starting to explore the idea that the psychological lows that follow the arrival of a baby

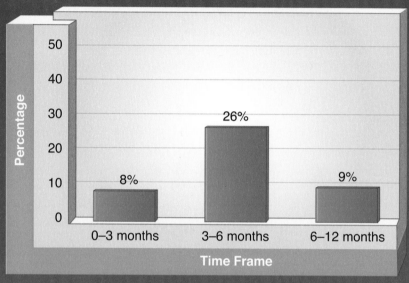

Rates of Paternal Depression Highest When Baby Is Three to Six Months Old

8% 0–3 months
26% 3–6 months
9% 6–12 months

Percentage

Time Frame

Based on data from forty-three studies involving 28,004 participants published between 1980 and October 2009.

Taken from: James Paulson and Sharnail Bazemore. "Prenatal and Postpartum Depression in Fathers and its Association With Maternal Depression." *Journal American Medical Association (JAMA)*, May 19, 2010.

may sometimes result merely from the challenges of bringing her home. "The exposure to stress, the change in life, the change in role—men in the home with a new baby experience a lot of the same kinds of stresses that women experience," Paulson says. "So from that perspective, seeing that men, postpartum, get depressed more often is really no surprise." (Support for the idea that stress can cause the baby blues comes from studies that show, for instance, that new parents who lack social support, have marital troubles, or are struggling financially—among other factors—have a higher incidence of depression.)

One of the reasons that postpartum depression has garnered so much attention is because it can have serious consequences for children. The AAP's new report lists the many ways in which kids of depressed moms may be worse-off: They are more likely to have developmental delays, social and emotional difficulties, cognitive and language problems, and more.

Ripple Effects

The emerging work on fathers shows that depression in dads can have similar ripple effects. In his 2006 study, Paulson found that melancholy fathers were less likely to play with or read, sing, or tell stories to their babies. A follow-up study, published in 2009, shows that these behavioral changes can have long-term effects on child development. Sad dads read to their kids less frequently, and the less reading aloud that fathers did, the worse their 2-year-olds scored on vocabulary tests.

Other research, conducted by University of Oxford psychiatrist Paul Ramchandani, turned up evidence that children whose fathers were depressed during their early infancy were more likely to suffer from behavioral problems at age 3-and-a-half. In 2008, Ramchandani also showed that kids whose fathers suffered from depression when they were 8 weeks old were 66 percent more likely to suffer from a diagnosable psychiatric disorder at age 7.

FAST FACT

According to the organization Postpartum Men, at least one in ten fathers become depressed after the birth of their child.

Of course, children of depressed fathers are more likely to have some genetic risk for developing their own mood disorders. But there could easily be environmental mechanisms at work as well. "Depression affects how fathers interact with their children," Ramchandani says. "They may be more irritable, they may be more withdrawn. That might affect children's understanding of emotions and how they learn to regulate their own emotions." Mood problems may also influence fathers' ability to work, affect the strength of their marital relationships, and more—any of which could put their kids at risk.

It Is a Real Problem

The accumulated evidence is clear: Depression in new dads—whatever the name, whatever the mechanism—is a real problem. And we need to be more proactive about catching it. It's not necessarily an easy task. As the AAP recommendations demonstrate, doctors involved in pregnancy and childbirth are trained, for obvious reasons, to focus on the health of mother and child. In Britain, however, physicians are starting to consider the missing family member: the father. In a pilot program launched at a hospital in Essex, England, the nurses and midwives in the maternity ward screen new dads, as well as moms, for signs of mood problems, both during pregnancy and after childbirth. Experienced dads have also been trained to run a fathers-only telephone helpline. It's a simple intervention and a good place to start.

The AAP's paper could have provided the impetus for doctors and hospitals in the United States to start taking similar action. Instead, it continued the not-so-grand tradition of ignoring dads.

Post-Adoption Depression Is Similar to Postpartum Depression

Karen J. Foli, interview by Meredith Resnick

In the following viewpoint social worker and health writer Meredith Resnick asks Karen J. Foli about post-adoption depression (PAD). Foli, who has studied PAD extensively, says adoptive moms, as well as dads, can suffer from depression after bringing a newly adopted child home. The pressures of the adoption process, feelings of inadequacy, and fears of not bonding with their children may contribute to PAD, says Foli. Foli is an assistant professor at the Purdue School of Nursing.

Karen Foli, PhD, and John Thompson, MD, are co-authors of the book *The Post-Adoption Blues*. Dr. Foli, a registered nurse, and her husband, John R. Thompson, a psychiatrist, have two children by birth and are themselves adoptive parents.

Dr. Foli, who is on the faculty at Purdue University, interviewed 21 adoptive parents about their adoption and depression experiences following the adoption, as well as

11 experts, professionals in the field of adoption. The adopted children's range of age at placement was newborn to 12 years—the research was conducted when the children were between 12 months to 24 years respectively. Foli's findings were published in the March 2009 issue of *Western Journal of Nursing Research.*

According to Dr. Foli, "Many adoptive parents spend their time during the adoption process demonstrating they are not only going to be fit parents, but super parents, and then they struggle with trying to be the world's best parent when the child is placed in the home. . . . Adoptive parents also may experience feelings about their legitimacy as a parent, or even surprise if they don't readily bond with the infant or child."

Dr. Foli took some time out to answer some questions about depression following an adoption.

Adoptive parents' expectations can be a factor in post-adoption depression because they may represent an unrealistic view of parenthood. But, like all parents, they may struggle with feelings of legitimacy as parents and may have trouble bonding with the child. (© Penny Tweedie/Photo Researchers, Inc.)

Meredith: What are some signs of post-adoption depression that may not seem obvious to new moms and dads? What are the most obvious signs?

Dr. Foli: The signs of postadoption depression are clinical signs of depression. According to the *Diagnostic and Statistical Manual* (Fourth Edition), the book that professionals use to diagnose individuals, the signs and symptoms of depression include:

- A depressed mood; feeling sad or empty
- Loss of interest or pleasure
- Significant (unintended) weight loss or weight gain
- Difficulty sleeping or wanting to sleep all the time
- Feeling like you can't sit still/restless, or feel like you're slowed down/can't physically get going
- Fatigue or loss of energy
- Feelings of worthlessness or excessive guilt
- Diminished ability to think or concentrate or indecisiveness
- Recurrent thoughts of death or thinking about suicide/acting on these thoughts
- Five of the nine symptoms above should be present for the past two weeks and at least one of these five symptoms should include depressed mood or loss of interest or pleasure.

That being said, there might be other problems such as difficulty bonding with the child and the "typical" transition to parenting might be prolonged and exaggerated. There might be feelings of anxiety and even a "panic" that could be related to depression or other mental health issues.

Can dads experience this post-partum/adoptive depression as well?

Yes. The literature supports that there are "sad" birth fathers.

The research I have conducted which surrounds adoptive fathers also indicates that fathers may struggle with depression as well. The signs and symptoms of depression,

Adoptive Parents' Expectations

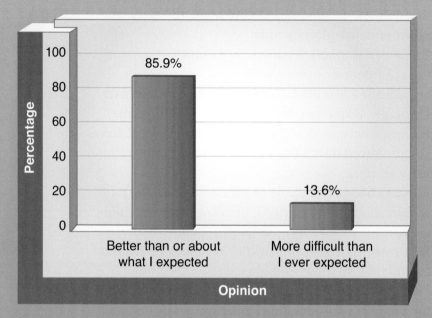

"So far how has having your child in your life compared with what you thought it would be like?"

85.9%

13.6%

Better than or about what I expected

More difficult than I ever expected

Percentage

Opinion

Based on data from the National Survey of Adoptive Parents, 2007–2009.

Taken from: Karen J. Foli. "Depression in Adoptive Parents: A Model of Understanding Through Grounded Theory." *Western Journal of Nursing Research*, published online December 29, 2009.

however, might vary from the mothers. For example, fathers may be more disengaged, angry, frustrated, and cope by spending more time at work, etc. We still have much to understand about this area.

What does treatment for PAD look like? What does it entail—and what can parents expect? Does it have to include medication?

The interventions to help alleviate depression with adoptive parents are very individualized. For example, one mother who took great pleasure in her career was advised to stay home with her baby daughter and take an extended leave from work. This mom was also exhausted emotionally after the adoption process. But what was highly valued in her life had been disrupted. She eventually found a good therapist that she could talk with and secured the services of an excellent daycare for her daughter and returned to work. She rebounded from her depression, bonded with her child and was able to heal. It took a lot of work on her part, and finding a therapist who was "adoption smart" wasn't easy. But she did it.

Do babies pick up on the mom's depression? How would a parent recognize this—and what should a parent do?

I think the question is really: What are the outcomes for a child who has one or both parents who are [depressed]? We know from the postpartum literature that there are significant negative outcomes experienced by children who have a depressed parent(s). There has been one study with adoptive parents as well and we find similar effects. Indeed, one could argue that children who are adopted are more vulnerable and are experiencing a tremendous adjustment period. Parental depression's effect on the child is an important reason to find effective treatments for the parents and why I can't emphasize to parents enough that by helping themselves, they're helping their children and families.

CHAPTER 3

Personal Experiences with Postpartum Depression

Living Through Postpartum Psychosis

Sarah R. Fields

In the following viewpoint Sarah R. Fields describes her traumatic ordeal of suffering from postpartum psychosis after the birth of her second child. Fields describes being delusional and afraid she could harm her children. Slowly, with conventional and homeopathic treatments, and the support of her family, Fields regained her sanity. During her ordeal she continued to breast-feed her children and believes this was important for her and her baby. After her recovery, Fields started a support group for women diagnosed with mood disorders associated with childbirth. Fields is from Indiana.

She's so fragile. I could kill her without trying. I realized this when my daughter, Anna, was born. Such innocence and utter dependence! Two years later, the arrival of my son, John, brought a return of the same fears. What if I dropped him down the stairs? Becoming a mother brings a sense of reverence and holy fear, in the

Photo on opposite page. Several studies find that for every 1,000 pregnant women, 1 or 2 will develop postpartum psychosis within two to four weeks after delivery. (© Ian Hooten/ Photo Researchers, Inc.)

face of the awesome responsibility of caring for a tiny little life. Sometimes, when a mother loses touch with reality, those fears come true.

When I learned, from one study, that one in 25 mothers with postpartum psychosis kills her child, I was overwhelmed with a feeling of gratitude. Postpartum psychosis affects only one to two women per thousand in the first year after giving birth, but when my son was six months old, it happened to me. No harm came to either of my children while I was psychotic, thanks to close supervision and quick intervention by my husband and my parents. But I realize now that it could have.

A Sense of Impending Doom

The problem began with a bout of depression, due in part to social isolation and in part to grief: We were living in a new community, and my father-in-law was dying of Alzheimer's. I was able to cope as long as Carl, my husband, was home from school for the summer, but when he returned to teaching in the fall and left me home alone during the day with two-and-a-half-year-old Anna and five-month-old John, I found myself swinging from inexplicable sorrow to blinding rage and back again. I lost my appetites for food and sex. After a month or so of skipping breakfast, I also stopped eating lunch, and found myself tandem-nursing two children on one meal a day. Even when I tried to sleep at night, I couldn't relax. Carl would wake in the wee hours to find me reading a book by a tiny night-light as the children dozed beside me.

I felt a sense of impending doom, and was plagued by severe guilt that I could neither explain nor escape. That feeling of guilt was the worst part of my depression: I felt as if I carried the weight of the world in my soul. When Katrina struck a thousand miles from our house, I felt as if the hurricane had barreled through my body and left me drowning in its wake.

Some mothers experience profound guilt, periods of anger and anxiety, and a sense of impending doom after the birth of a second child. (© **Sharpenson Ltd/Photo Researchers, Inc.**)

A series of shocks left my frayed nerves totally jangled. We were struck by a drunk driver in a hit-and-run accident, and just days later, in a hotel, we were awakened at three in the morning by a security guard, who asked us to leave because the hotel management thought we hadn't paid for the room. After that, I didn't sleep for four nights. My next sleep would come in a psychiatric hospital.

Delusions

Over the two days following the hotel incident, I became increasingly delusional and suspicious of my loved ones. My behavior was strange: I ran into a convenience store hollering about abortion; I refused to feed my daughter during the day; I asked my neighbor to leave my house because I was convinced she was trying to kidnap the children and make them part of a cult; I accused Carl of having affairs with all our friends. By the second day, Carl realized that I could not be left alone, and drove me to my parents' house, two states away. I wandered down the highway by their house in sub-freezing temperatures with no coat, convinced I'd seen a friend from home who was there to rescue me from the imaginary cult. I scanned magazines because I believed they were full of codes placed there just for me. Clues in the everyday world pointed to my theories: When Mom loaned me a coat with a cassette tape in the pocket, I took this as evidence that the FBI was tapping my phone calls.

The day after we arrived at my parents' house (still no sleep), we went as a family to see a psychiatric nurse practitioner. During the appointment, I couldn't sit still. I frantically cleaned her office while my parents and husband talked with her. I decided that the nurse practitioner was actually the lesbian lover of my 90-year-old grandmother (who lived with my parents), and accused her of trying to dominate me. She told my family that the hospital didn't have a free bed until the next day, and sent us home to wait. During the night, convinced that my grandmother was going to swallow all her pills at once to kill herself, I placed myself on "suicide watch." I screamed for hours as Carl and my father physically restrained me so that I wouldn't keep jumping in bed with her to keep her from killing herself. Twice that night I called the police to tell them I was guilty of murdering my grandmother because I couldn't prevent her suicide. Grandma took out her hearing aids and went to sleep, but I was sore and hoarse for three days. The police did come by twice in the night to check on the house, and Mom asked them to come back the next day to help get me into the car to go to the hospital. They did.

On the way to the hospital, Carl sat beside me in the back seat of my parents' van and held my hand, fearing I might try to jump out of the moving vehicle. During check-in, I threatened to sue the hospital. A nurse tried to gather my medical history from me and my dad as the psychiatrist interviewed my mother and husband about my background and symptoms. Mom, a retired La Leche League Leader, explained in no uncertain terms that I would want to continue breastfeeding. The nurse brought me a breast pump, but neither she nor I could figure out how to use it.

The Psychiatric Ward

Carl left with my parents, taking the children, and I was alone. I thought I recognized many of the patients there, and called them by the names I thought were theirs. I was sure we were in a concentration camp, or in hell. The hospital staff took away my shoes and removed the hangers from the closet, for fear I would hang myself, and locked up the bag Carl had packed. I had nothing of my own.

I accused the psychiatrist of trying to rape the patients, and insisted that a female nurse be present during my first meeting with him. I spoke in an accusatory tone about conspiracies, lawsuits, and codes, but was able to momentarily "hide" my psychosis when I wanted to—for instance, when I spoke about breastfeeding. I told the doctor that I wanted to nurse, and asked him to go to La Leche League's website for help in allowing me to do so. I quoted a friend, La Leche League Leader Pam Ahearn, who said that "healing begins at the breast." I suggested the doctor read Dr. Thomas W. Hale's book, *Medications and Mothers' Milk*, as he considered psychiatric drugs for me. When he came back the next day with the book, I began to accept him.

That first evening in the hospital, I trusted the patients more than the staff. I followed one patient—an elderly woman with an eye infection who spoke nonsensical phrases over and over—sure that she was my long-dead paternal grandmother. When she needed help in the bathroom, I tried to break in, now sure that the nurses were going to rape her. As I yanked on the bathroom door, five gloved security guards grabbed me and pinned me down on the bed in the isolation room. As I screamed "You're killing me! I can't believe you're killing me!" a nurse pulled down my pants and gave me an injection in the butt. I put my head down to die. It was the first sleep I'd had in four days.

I woke at four in the morning and asked for my son. We had never been separated before, and my breasts were so full they felt as if they would explode. Carl arrived with John, who nursed contentedly after having cried all night and refused formula. What a relief to hold my baby again, to feed him in my arms and be soothed by his presence as he was comforted at my breast. That morning, the psychiatrist gave permission for John to stay in the hospital with me, as long as Carl stayed, too, to take responsibility for the baby's safety. We pushed two hospital beds together to make a "family bed" in the locked-down psychiatric ward. The doctor asked where John would sleep. Although I knew John would be in bed with me, and although I wasn't sure what it was, I asked for an isolette. (I knew it was some type of hospital baby bed.) The nurse wheeled into my room a twin bed with a cage around it—a giant crib. I was convinced that the hospital was going to remove my vital organs and deposit my corpse in this terrifying contraption. Instead, it served as a makeshift dresser for the nine days we spent in the hospital.

We then fell into a rhythm, as I began to make up for lost sleep and missed meals. I devoured as much food as the hospital kitchen sent up to my room. Every hour during the night, a nurse would peek into our room—the lights were never completely switched off—to check on me. The psychiatrist prescribed one dose per day of antipsychotic medication instead of two, to be taken just before bed so that the levels would peak in my bloodstream

FAST FACT

According to several studies, for every 1,000 women who give birth, 1–2 of them will develop postpartum psychosis within the first two to four weeks after delivery.

—and in my milk—as John and I slept. My parents and my daughter, Anna, visited me each afternoon. Anna nursed when we were together—it was hard to reconnect so briefly. She coslept with my parents at night, but it would be months before she felt relaxed and happy again. For those months, she worried about my becoming sick again and returning to the hospital.

I was released on a pass for six hours on Thanksgiving Day, and the following Saturday I left the hospital. The medicine left me sleepy, and I walked around stiffly, holding my arms in front of me, like a zombie. I ate every meal as if it were my last. After two weeks at my parents' house, we went home, and Mom stayed with us that first week. Then friends from church took turns coming by every day for a few weeks.

Peace and Healing Arrives

After I returned home from Wisconsin in December, I contacted Dr. Karl Robinson, a homeopathic physician, who treated me with a constitutional homeopathic remedy. For the first time in months, I was able to relate to people without fear, to be alone without feeling panic, and to renew the bond of family with my children and husband. While conventional psychiatric medicine helped me to sleep at first, I believe it was homeopathy that brought me true peace and healing. The constitutional treatment gave me the power to pursue dreams and ambitions that had been buried by self-doubt and inertia.

During those weeks before Christmas, Dr. Brian McGuckin, our family chiropractor, tested my blood for nutrient levels and found me very deficient, especially in iron and calcium. He prescribed 15 different vitamins and minerals in high doses, to allow my adrenal glands to rest, and to nourish my cells. The supplements calmed me and brought color back to my skin. Within a week I felt more energetic and able to cope.

In January, at a local domestic violence shelter, I began attending a series of support-group meetings for survivors of sexual assault. While attending college overseas almost a decade before, I had been raped. Sexual abuse can be a risk factor for postpartum mood disorders, and I realized that I had never resolved the feelings of shame and guilt stemming from the assault. Over the next nine months, I was slowly weaned off the medications.

Music has always been a source of nourishment for my soul, so I began singing again. I wrote letters and made phone calls to old friends. Finding support in those who had brought me comfort in my childhood and early adulthood satisfied a deep need for connection with others. I joined a playgroup for mothers and children and am now active in encouraging mothers in my town to consider practicing attachment parenting, as they in turn teach me about tolerance of mothering styles that differ from mine. I reawakened an interest in writing, and joined a writers' group to learn to let my heart sing by telling stories and writing poems, and making a record of my memories.

Just this year, I started a local mother-to-mother support group for mothers diagnosed with perinatal mood disorders, including postpartum depression and psychosis—because while I was healing, what most helped me was talking with women who had been there, and who promised me that I would be well and would soon feel like myself again.

Breastfeeding Was Important

Psychosis was terrifying for me and for my family, and healing took months. Finding an outpatient psychiatrist who would allow me to continue nursing my son was a challenge, but I insisted on protecting our nursing relationship. I am very grateful to La Leche League for the publications, philosophy, and people who provided me with the courage to continue nursing despite the obstacle of a psychotic episode. Nursing kept my babies safe when I became psychotic, because even when my mind was scattered to the four winds, my body remembered how to do what mothers do. Even when my mental state was chaotic, my heart guided my arms and breasts to surround, nurture, and protect my children. They are alive today because my body remembered how to care for them, and took over for me.

Ready for New Baby

It is over a year now since I became psychotic, and I have had no relapse in symptoms. We found out last Christmas that we are expecting our third child, and I am overjoyed with the news. I feel confident that by maintaining good nutrition and sleep habits, implementing preventive measures, getting comprehensive blood work done by my health care provider, and remaining under the watchful eye of my family and midwife, psychosis will not happen to me again. If it does, I'm ready with a treatment plan, care providers, well-informed friends and family, and the wisdom that comes from experience.

My Journey Through Postpartum Depression

Marie Osmond

In the following viewpoint entertainer Marie Osmond describes her battle with postpartum depression (PPD). Osmond details the symptoms that indicated to her something was wrong following the birth of her child: She could not sleep, her heart would race while being physically exhausted, and involuntary spasms would take over her legs and muscles. Osmond claims when she looked at herself in the mirror, it was as if a stranger was glaring back. Osmond urges those dealing with postpartum depression or those who know of someone dealing with it to seek treatment immediately.

I can sleep anywhere. I think this ability evolved during my childhood while touring the world with my brothers and performing as the Osmonds. I've always defined a bed as any surface that would allow me to put my head down. I've curled up on an instrument case, across the

SOURCE: Marie Osmond, "'I Had Lost All Joy and Hope': My Personal Battle Against PPD," *Newsweek*, July 2, 2001. Reproduced by permission.

luggage rack of a Greyhound bus and next to a backstage costume rack, with my head propped against a hoop skirt.

Being unable to sleep following the birth of my last baby gave me the first clue that something was wrong. I would lie down, exhausted, but my heart would be racing as fast as my mind. Then my whole physical being would get in the act: my hands trembling, my stomach in spasms, my legs twitching involuntarily and my head and neck throbbing in pain to a rhythm I had never felt before. Taking a deep breath was a challenge.

My emotions were like a maddening game of Marco Polo. They seemed to break through the surface, sending me blindly off in an attempt to regain control, unable to catch up before they would resurface in a totally different direction.

When I saw myself in the mirror, it felt as if I were looking at the face of a stranger. My eyes were lifeless and hollow. I had lost all joy, and any hope had diminished to a distant memory. I literally could not recognize myself. Postpartum depression had stripped me of the very core of my being. Nothing seemed steadfast. I felt utterly alone.

I gave birth to my baby in July [1999]. I was unable to seek the help I truly needed until November.

I watched the news on Thursday morning as the image was played over and over again of Andrea Yates being led to a police car in handcuffs after she confessed to drowning her five small children. I wondered, if she had been watching the same footage, would she have recognized herself? I would guess not.

In my experience with postpartum depression I never had any thoughts of harming my children. I'm grateful I was spared those feelings. But I spent five months in the darkest place I've ever been. I'm a woman who had available resources, close friends and family, a present and loving husband and the financial ability to seek out assistance. With access to all this, I still put on the face of

Despite experiencing severe symptoms of postpartum depression, Marie Osmond (pictured) waited several months before speaking out. (© AP Images/Universal Orlando, Kevin Kolczynski)

being in control. I still insisted to anyone who asked that I was "fine."

Why did I do that? Looking back, I can give two reasons. The first is shame. I couldn't admit to anyone, even my husband, that I was having a hard time coping. How do you express that you are in complete despair when everything you've been told or seen in the media represents new motherhood as the happiest, most fulfilling time in a woman's life? How could I admit to my doctor that I couldn't seem to control my emotions and that my physical body was foreign to me? I didn't know anyone else who felt this way. Who, then, would understand?

The second reason is immobilization. This is the harshest reality of depression. I couldn't make a move on my own. Depression robbed me of any energy it would take to make an extra phone call, get an appointment or even try to explain how I felt.

When I finally did make the call, I was fortunate enough to find a doctor who understood, who listened without judgment and took on the responsibility of helping me when I couldn't help myself. She explained and examined my symptoms; she consulted and comforted my feelings. She educated me on the reasons for PPD, from the hormonal factors to the physiological factors to the psychological factors. Most important, I received the proper tests and the treatments I needed, included counseling.

My parents' generation would refer to pregnancy as a woman being in a "delicate condition." I feel that the most delicate condition starts after the baby is born. We need to dispel the motherhood myth and acknowledge that a woman is undergoing a time of incredible biological, emotional and personal change. This is not a time to send her on her way 24 hours after giving birth to care for an infant who needs around-the-clock care. I encourage anyone who knows a woman with young children to check in with her.

Even if she insists she's "fine," follow through with her. Don't let the days pass. Time is critical, because if she is suffering symptoms of postpartum depression, the sooner she can receive treatment, the sooner she will be able to cope. Make the phone call for her. If one doctor doesn't seem to understand, find another one for her. It's an act of love that could be lifesaving.

FAST FACT

According to Postpartum Progress, the first year postpartum has the highest divorce rate than any other time during a marriage.

I sleep much better now. The physical symptoms of my postpartum depression are gone, and the emotional issues, though I still have bad days, are finding a resolution. I'm certain a resolution is much further away for Russell Yates [Andrea Yates's husband]. His loss is unimaginable. Not only are his little children no longer with him, but it appears he lost his wife to postpartum depression.

Before I put my head down to sleep this week, I will bow it in prayer, along with the rest of the country, and ask that out of the agony of this tragedy there will come a purpose.

A Dad Talks About Having Postpartum Depression

Joel Schwartzberg

In the following viewpoint Joel Schwartzberg asserts that men can get postpartum depression too. Schwartzberg says he fell into a deep depression after the birth of his son. Years later he was surprised to learn that he had suffered from male postpartum depression. It helped, said Schwartzberg, to know that there was an explanation for his behavior and that he was not alone. Schwartzberg is an award-winning humorist, essayist, and screenwriter whose work has appeared in *Newsweek*, the *New York Times Magazine*, and many other publications. His 2009 book *The 40-Year-Old Version: Humoirs of a Divorced Dad* provides a collection of his essays.

I thought being a dad would come easily to me. But soon after my son's birth, I was looking for a way out.

Nearly every night of the first few weeks of my son's life, I'd click him into the back seat of our minivan and drive him around until he fell asleep. Like so many babies lulled by the humming of tires on pavement, the kid conked out in 10 minutes, but I'd continue on to the closest Dunkin' Donuts with an all-night drive-thru window, nearly an hour away.

My wife and I made this arrangement to allow her some precious sleep, but as I volunteered for chauffeur duty again and again—each time coming home later and later—we both knew there was more going on than her exhaustion and my craving for doughnuts.

In the parking lot, I would pray my son would stay asleep and not set my already-frayed nerves on fire. I'd cram those doughnuts into my mouth as if they were the last delicious things on earth.

The author relates his own experiences with postpartum depression. Here, he holds his daughter at a holiday event. (© AP Images/Mike Derer)

These were the tiny, fleeting pleasures I clung to after my son was born. They felt like all I had left. When a child was added to my life, it was as if something enormous and coveted was subtracted in return, and the transaction left me reeling, like someone who'd just gambled away his soul.

I fell into a well of depression so deep I wasn't even aware of it. It was only years later, after I spoke to a psychotherapist, that I learned I was experiencing male postpartum depression. It seems ridiculous on its face: men don't do the hard work of carrying a pregnancy for nine months. We don't have to bear the pains of labor. We never had an umbilical connection to our children. We just have to hang on tight. But giving my emotions a name, and an explanation, helped me feel less alone and better able to cut myself some slack. Before then, even calling it depression felt like an excuse for weak, pathetic behavior.

> **FAST FACT**
>
> Studies show that men are more likely than women to try to hide their depression or to withdraw from others.

This was not what I expected from fatherhood. I was 31 and thought I'd slide into it easily. "What's a little sleep deprivation?" parents-to-be tell themselves. We got through college, after all. But not 48 hours after we returned home with our boy, a truth dawned on me with shocking force: my life was gone. Movies, sleeping, long showers—all gone. We became slaves to this tiny new thing living in our home, and there was no going back.

I ceded nearly complete authority to my wife, then blamed both her and my son for my feelings of loss and insignificance. I took on every parental responsibility with sucked-up reluctance on the outside and contempt on the inside. My wife seemed to consider me selfish and irresponsible. She was tired, she'd say, of parenting both of us. Even when the bickering ended, the wounds never healed. Our marriage took a fatal hit.

I couldn't mask my sadness when my work colleagues asked excitedly about fatherhood. "It's good . . . well, it's

OK," I said. "Actually, it's very, very hard." By then, I was close to tears. We were all happy when the conversation ended. Later on, they told me I'd scared the crap out of them. I'm sure at least a few went back on contraception.

One day, I sat on the hardwood floor next to my son, both of us exhausted. My son started crying. Then I did, too. Actually, we bawled. I don't know why he was crying, but I was mourning the loss of my life as I knew it. As messy as it was, that shared sob was our first moment of bonding, and it helped steer me toward responsibility.

Eventually, my wife and I divorced, but our split actually enhanced my relationship with my kids. (We had twin girls after my son.) It forced me to locate my inner parent, the one who tells me when it's OK to let my son stay up late, when it's appropriate to be interrupted on the phone by a whining daughter and whether a tense situation calls for stern rules or just an all-out, friendly family wrestling match.

Nine years later, I look back at an old photo of my son and me asleep together on a sunlit bed when he was a newborn. Our faces are peaceful and our arms stretched upward, as if we're doing a stadium wave. I view the picture as incontrovertible evidence that he was a part of me—a time-sucking, sleep-stealing, delicious part of me. And what's more, he needed me. I just had to step outside of myself to see it. I was no less a dad all along, just a lost one.

GLOSSARY

affective disorder   A mental disorder involving abnormal moods and emotions.

antenatal depression   Depression that some women feel while they are pregnant.

anticonvulsants   Medicines used to prevent seizures that are sometimes prescribed for depression or depression-related illnesses.

antidepressants   A category of medications used to treat depression.

anxiety disorder   An illness that produces an intense, often unrealistic and excessive state of apprehension and fear. This may or may not occur during or in anticipation of a specific situation, and may be accompanied by a rise in blood pressure, increased heart rate, rapid breathing, nausea, and other signs of agitation or discomfort.

baby blues   A brief period of mild depression occurring in new moms during the first days or weeks after birth.

bipolar disorder   A mental illness that causes people to have severe high and low moods. People with this illness switch from feeling overly happy and joyful (or irritable) to feeling overly sad and hopeless. In between mood swings, a person's moods may be normal.

cognitive behavioral therapy   A form of psychotherapy that emphasizes the important role of a person's thoughts in how that person feels and what he or she does.

delusion   A false belief that is resistant to reason or contrary to actual fact.

depression   A clinical mood disorder associated with low mood or loss of interest and other symptoms that prevent a person from leading a normal life.

DSM-IV   The 1994 revision of the *Diagnostic and Statistical Manual of Mental Disorders*, which is published by the American Psychiatric Association and provides a common language and standard criteria for the classification of mental disorders.

dysphoric mood	Low mood that may include dissatisfaction, restlessness, or depression.
dysthymia	Also sometimes referred to as chronic depression. This type of depression mostly occurs over a period of at least two years in adults and one year in children and adolescents. It is characterized by less severe, lingering symptoms of depression that may last for years.
Edinburgh Postnatal Depression Scale	A ten-item questionnaire developed specifically to identify women who have postpartum depression.
hallucination	The perception of something that does not exist. Examples of hallucinations are hearing voices when no one is speaking, seeing something that is not there, or smelling something that is not present.
infanticide	The killing of an infant.
major depressive disorder	A type of mood disorder characterized by one or more major depressive episodes. Major depressive disorder is not diagnosed if the syndrome is attributable to an acute grief reaction or a nonaffective psychotic condition such as schizophrenia.
meta-analysis	A systematic method that takes data from a number of independent studies and integrates them using statistical analysis.
neurosis	A relatively mild mental illness that is not caused by organic disease, involving symptoms of stress (depression, anxiety) but not a loss of touch with reality.
panic disorder	An anxiety disorder in which a person suffers from sudden attacks of fear and panic. Symptoms of the attacks include rapid heartbeat, chest sensations, shortness of breath, dizziness, tingling, and feeling anxious.
parturition	The act of childbirth.
perinatal depression	A condition encompassing major and minor depressive episodes that occur during pregnancy (prenatal) or within the first twelve months following delivery (postpartum).

phobia	An anxiety disorder in which a person suffers from an unusual amount of fear of a certain activity or situation.
postpartum	Typically the period from parturition to twelve months after delivery.
postpartum depression	A moderate to severe depression in a woman after she has given birth. It may occur soon after delivery or up to a year later. Most of the time, it occurs within the first three months after delivery.
postpartum disorder	A range of emotional, physical, and behavioral changes that may be experienced by new mothers.
postpartum psychosis	Also known as puerperal psychosis, this condition is a severe and rare postpartum disorder, affecting 1 to 2 women per 1,000 births. Women with postpartum psychosis present with new onset of delusions or prominent hallucinations.
prenatal	The period of pregnancy from conception to parturition.
progesterone	A female hormone produced by the ovaries. Progesterone, along with estrogen, prepares the uterus (womb) for a possible pregnancy each month and supports the fertilized egg if conception occurs. Progesterone also helps prepare the breasts for milk production and breast-feeding.
psychiatrist	A medical doctor who treats mental illness. Psychiatrists must receive additional training and serve a supervised residency in their specialty. They can prescribe medications.
psychologist	A professional who treats mental illness, emotional disturbance, and behavior problems using talk therapy. Psychologists cannot prescribe medication.
psychosis	A severe mental disorder in which thought and emotions are so impaired that contact is lost with external reality.
psychosocial	A term used to describe the influence of social factors on mental health and behavior.
psychotherapy	The treatment of mental disorder by psychological rather than medical means.

puerperal   Relating to, or occurring during, childbirth or the period immediately following.

puerperal fever   A form of septicemia (infection) generally caused by *streptococ-
cus*, accompanied by fever, in which the focus of the infection is
the uterus.

sedative   A drug that calms and allows a person to sleep.

selective serotonin   A class of antidepressant drugs that help to increase serotonin, a
reuptake inhibitors   chemical responsible for communication between nerves in the
(SSRIs)   brain.

trimester   One of the three three-month periods of a pregnancy—the first,
second, or third trimester.

CHRONOLOGY

ca. 460 B.C.	Ancient Greek physicianHippocrates describes postpartum "fever," which produces "agitation, delirium and attacks of mania."
ca. A.D. 1000's	Italian gynecologist Trotula writes that "if the womb is too moist, the brain is filled with water, and the moisture running over to the eyes, compels them to involuntarily shed tears."
1829	English physician Robert Gooch writes *The Account of Some of the Most Important Diseases Peculiar to Women.*
1838	French psychiatrist Jean-Etienne Dominique Esquirol reports on the systematic study of mental illness related to childbirth.
1846–1864	English asylum superintendents John Charles Bucknill and William Hack Tuke note that a large proportion of admissions to insane asylums are linked to pregnancy, birth, and lactation.
1858	French physician Louis-Victor Marcé publishes the *Treatise on Insanity in Pregnant and Lactating Women.*
1895	English psychiatrist Henry Maudsley's book *Psychology of the Mind* identifies two types of insanity associated with pregnancy.
1922	England passes the Infanticide Act, which recognizes the time surrounding childbirth as biologically vulnerable and makes infanticide a less severe crime.
1968	The second edition of the *Diagnostic and Statistical Manual of Mental Disorders* (*DSM-II*) describes "Psychosis with Childbirth" as a separate entity.
1980	The third edition of the *Diagnostic and Statistical Manual of Mental Disorders* (*DSM-III*) eliminates "Psychosis with Childbirth" as a separate category, stating, "There is no compelling evidence that postpartum psychosis is a distinct entity."

1987   English psychiatrist John Cox and his colleagues develop a depression screening questionnaire specifically for women in the postpartum period.

1994   The fourth edition of the *Diagnostic and Statistical Manual of Mental Disorders* (*DSM-IV*) defines major depression with postpartum onset as episodes of depression occurring in a woman beginning within four weeks of giving birth.

2001   Andrea Yates drowns her five children in the bathtub of her Houston, Texas, home. The incident focuses public attention on postpartum depression and postpartum psychosis.

2003   The Melanie Blocker-Stokes Postpartum Depression Research and Care Act is first introduced in the US Congress.

2010   The Melanie Blocker Stokes Act becomes law.

ORGANIZATIONS TO CONTACT

The editors have compiled the following list of organizations concerned with the issues debated in this book. The descriptions are derived from materials provided by the organizations. All have publications or information available for interested readers. The list was compiled on the date of publication of the present volume; the information provided here may change. Be aware that many organizations take several weeks or longer to respond to inquiries, so allow as much time as possible.

American College of Obstetricians and Gynecologists (ACOG)
409 12th St. SW,
PO Box 96920,
Washington, DC
20090-6920
(202) 638-5577
website: www.acog
.org

ACOG is a nonprofit organization of professionals providing health care for women. ACOG advocates for quality health care for women, promotes patient education, and increases awareness among its members and the public of the changing issues facing women's health care. ACOG issues important guidelines and bulletins and publishes several journals such as *Obstetrics & Gynecology* and *Special Issues in Women's Health*.

American Psychiatric Association (APA)
1000 Wilson Blvd.,
Ste. 1825, Arlington,
VA 22209-3901
(888) 357-7924
e-mail: apa@psych.org
website: www.psych
.org

The APA is an organization of professionals working in the field of psychiatry. The APA works to advance the profession and promote the highest quality care for individuals with mental illnesses and their families. Additionally, the APA educates the public about mental health, psychiatry, and successful treatment options. The organization publishes the twice-monthly newsletter *Psychiatric News* as well as several journals, including the *American Journal of Psychiatry* and *Psychiatric Services*.

Childbirth and Postpartum Professional Association (CAPPA)
PO Box 2406,
Buford, GA 30515
(888) 692-2772
fax: (888) 688-5241
e-mail: info@cappa.net
website: www.cappa.net

CAPA offers comprehensive, evidence-based education, certification, professional membership, and training to childbirth educators, lactation educators, labor doulas, antepartum doulas, and postpartum doulas worldwide. CAPPA-certified professionals aim to facilitate empowerment, connection, and self-advocacy in families from preconception through early parenthood. CAPPA seeks to forge positive and productive relationships between organizations that support healthy, informed family choices. The organization consists of a leadership board, regional representatives, trainers, mentors, advisers, and its membership.

Childbirth Connection
260 Madison Ave.,
8th Fl., New York, NY 10016
(212) 777-5000
fax: (212) 777-9320
e-mail: www.childbirthconnection.org
website: www.childbirthconnection.org

Childbirth Connection is a national nonprofit organization dedicated to improving the quality and value of maternity care through consumer engagement and health system transformation. The organization promotes safe, effective, and satisfying evidence-based maternity care for all women and families. Childbirth Connection publications include *Childbirth Connection eNews* and the *Listening to Mothers Survey Report*. Many other reports, brochures, and fact sheets are available on the organization's website.

International Association for Women's Mental Health (IAWMH)
8213 Lakenheath Way, Potomac, MD 20854
(301) 983-6282
fax: (301) 983-6288
e-mail: info@iawmh.org
website: www.iawmh.org

The IAWMH is a nonprofit organization that seeks to improve the mental health of women throughout the world, to expand the fund of knowledge about women's mental health, and to promote gender-sensitive and autonomy-enhancing mental health services for women. Each year the IAWMH sponsors the World Congress on Women's Mental Health, which brings together women's health professionals from around the world to discuss the psychosocial, biological, and clinical aspects of women's mental health from individual, family, community, society, and global perspectives.

Mental Health America
2000 N. Beauregard St., 6th Fl., Alexandria, VA 22311
(703) 684-7722
fax: (703) 684-5968
e-mail: infoctr@mentalhealthamerica.net
website: www.mentalhealthamerica.net

Mental Health America (formerly known as the National Mental Health Association) is a nonprofit organization dedicated to helping all people live mentally healthier lives. The organization educates the public about ways to preserve and strengthen its mental health; fights for access to effective mental health care; seeks to end discrimination against people with mental and addictive disorders; and fosters innovative mental health research, treatment, and support services. Mental Health America issues several e-mail newsletters, such as the *Bell*, and produces several fact sheets and informational documents.

National Alliance on Mental Illness (NAMI)
2107 Wilson Blvd., Ste. 300, Arlington, VA 22201-3042
(703) 524-7600
fax: (703) 524-9094
e-mail: info@nami.org
website: www.nami.org

NAMI is a national grassroots mental health organization that seeks to eradicate mental illness and improve the lives of persons living with serious mental illness and their families. NAMI works through advocacy, research, education, and support. The organization publishes a periodic magazine called the *Advocate*.

National Institute of Mental Health (NIMH)
Science Writing, Press, and Dissemination Branch
6001 Executive Blvd., Rm. 8184, MSC 9663, Bethesda, MD 20892-9663
(866) 615-6464
fax: (301) 443-4279
e-mail: nimhinfo@nih.gov
website: www.nimh.nih.gov

NIMH is the leading agency of the US government concerned with mental health issues. The mission of NIMH is to reduce the burden of mental illness and behavioral disorders through research on mind, brain, and behavior. NIMH publishes various booklets, fact sheets, and easy-to-read materials on mental health issues.

Postpartum Support International (PSI)
6706 SW 54th Ave.,
Portland, OR 97219
(503) 894-9453
fax: (503) 894-9452
e-mail:
support@postpartum
.net
website: www
.postpartum.net

PSI is a nonprofit organization whose mission is to promote awareness, prevention, and treatment of mental health issues related to childbearing in every country worldwide. PSI's goal is that every woman and family worldwide will have access to information, social support, and informed professional care to deal with mental health issues related to childbearing. PSI promotes this vision through advocacy and collaboration, and by educating and training the professional community and the public. The organization provides a newsletter with up-to-date information on worldwide news, conferences, resources, research, and events.

US Department of Health and Human Services Office on Women's Health (OWH)
200 Independence Ave. SW, Rm. 712E, Washington, DC 20201
(202) 690-7650
e-mail: www.womens health.gov
website: www
.womenshealth.gov

The OHW within the US Department of Health and Human Services (HHS) was established in 1991 to improve the health of American women by advancing and coordinating a comprehensive women's health agenda throughout the HHS. The OWH achieves its mission and vision by developing innovative programs, educating health professionals, and motivating behavior change in consumers through the dissemination of health information. The OWH works with numerous government agencies, nonprofit organizations, consumer groups, and associations of health care professionals to promote health equity for women and girls through gender-specific approaches. The Women's Health website provides numerous publications about health care issues important to women.

FOR FURTHER READING

Books

Heather Armstrong, *It Sucked and Then I Cried: How I Had a Baby, a Breakdown, and a Much Needed Margarita.* New York: Gallery, 2010.

Shoshana Bennet and Pec Indman, *Beyond the Blues.* San Jose, CA: Moodswings, 2011.

Ariel Dalfen, *When Baby Brings the Blues: Solutions for Postpartum Depression.* Mississauga, ON: Wiley, 2009.

Arlene M. Huysman and Paul J. Goodnick, *Postpartum Effect: Deadly Depression in Mothers.* New York: Seven Stories, 2003.

Kathleen A. Kendall-Tackett, *Depression in New Mothers: Causes, Consequences, and Treatment Alternatives.* New York: Routledge, 2005.

Karen Kleiman and Amy Wenzel, *Dropping the Baby and Other Scary Thoughts: Breaking the Cycle of Unwanted Thoughts in Motherhood.* New York: Routledge, 2010.

Sylvia M. Lasalandra, *A Daughter's Touch: A Journey of a Mother Trying to Come to Terms with Postpartum Depression.* Toronto, ON: Quattro, 2005.

Adrienne Martini, *Hillbilly Gothic: A Memoir of Madness and Motherhood.* New York: Free Press, 2008.

Natasha S. Mauthner, *The Darkest Days of My Life: Stories of Postpartum Depression.* Cambridge, MA: Harvard University Press, 2002.

Susan McRoberts, *The Lifter of My Head: How God Sustained Me During Postpartum Depression.* Mustang, OK: Tate, 2007.

Michelle Olberman and Cheryl L. Meyer, *When Mothers Kill: Interviews from Prison*. New York: NYU Press, 2008.

Marie Osmond, *Behind the Smile: My Journey Out of Postpartum Depression*. New York: Warner, 2001.

Brooke Shields, *Down Came the Rain*. Los Angeles: Christa, 2006.

Teresa M. Twomey, *Understanding Postpartum Psychosis: A Temporary Madness*. Westport, CT: Praeger, 2009.

Joyce A. Venis, *Postpartum Depression Demystified: An Essential Guide for Understanding and Overcoming the Most Common Complication After Childbirth*. New York: Da Capo, 2007.

Tina Zahn and Wanda L. Dyson, *Why I Jumped: My True Story of Postpartum Depression, Dramatic Rescue & Return to Hope*. Grand Rapids, MI: Fleming H. Revell, 2006.

Periodicals

Dana Ballon, "Scared of the Sadness: Most New Moms Know About the Risk of Postpartum Depression," *Today's Parent*, November, 2007.

Melinda Beck, "Helping Kids Beat Depression—by Treating Mom," *Wall Street Journal*, May 17, 2011.

John Breeding and Amy Philo, "Open Letter to the Editor of Mothering Magazine—Re: 'Beat the Baby Blues,'" *Bitter Pill*, November 8, 2010.

Darcie Davis-Gage, Julie Jenks Kettman, and Joy Moel, "Developmental Transition of Motherhood: Treating Postpartum Depression Using a Feminist Approach," *Adultspan Journal*, Fall 2010.

Brian Doherty, "You Can't See Why on a fMRI: What Science Can, and Can't, Tell Us About the Insanity Defense," *Reason*, July, 2007.

Marian F. Earls and the Committee on Psychosocial Aspects of Child and Family, "Incorporating Recognition and Management of Perinatal and Postpartum Depression into Pediatric Practice," *Pediatrics*, October 25, 2010.

Alan W. Gemmill, Joshua Mendelsohn, and Jeannette Milgrom, "Does Postnatal Depression Screening Work? Throwing Out the Bathwater, Keeping the Baby," *Journal of Affective Disorders*, August 2011.

Caitlin Henderson and Jennifer Ribowsky, "Probing Postpartum Depression," *Clinician Reviews*, February 2011.

John Hoffman, "New Mom, New World: Life with Baby Can Be Difficult—It's Not a Weakness to Ask for Help," *Today's Parent*, April 2009.

Susan Hogan, "The Tyranny of the Maternal Body: Madness & Maternity," *Women's History Magazine*, Autumn 2006.

Ruth Davis Konigsberg, "A Wall of Silence," *Parents Magazine*, June 2011.

Gretel C. Kovach, "A Mother's Darkest Day," *Newsweek*, June 11, 2007.

Tina L. Liberto, "Screening for Depression and Help-Seeking in Postpartum Women During Well-Baby Pediatric Visits: An Integrated Review," *Journal of Pediatric Health Care*, August 12, 2010.

Susan London, "Family Violence Predicts Postpartum Depression," *Clinical Psychiatry News*, February 2011.

Hilary Marland, "Maternity and Madness: Puerperal Insanity in the Nineteenth Century," *UK Centre for the History of Nursing and Midwifery*, 2003.

Jason Meisner, "Woman Accused of Killing Son Had Severe Postpartum Depression, Lawyer Says," *Chicago Tribune*, April 14, 2011.

Partners in Discovery, "Pregnancy, Postpartum Depression and the Brain," Department of Neurology, University of California at Los Angeles, Fall 2009.

Melissa Lee Phillips, "Treating Postpartum Depression," *Monitor on Psychology*, February 2011.

Tiffany Rosenbrock, "Placenta Medicine: My Story," *Midwifery Today*, Winter 2008.

Dana Scarton, "Postpartum Depression Strikes New Dads as Well as Moms," *US News and World Report*, September 29, 2008.

Alexa Joy Sherman, "The Secret Sadness," *American Baby*, March 2011.

Pohla Smith, "Screening for Depression Before, During and After Pregnancy Can Help," *Pittsburgh Post-Gazette*, March 3, 2010.

Liz Szabo, "Postpartum Depression Hits as Many Dads as Moms," *USA Today*, May 19, 2010.

Karen Dineen Wagner, "Effects of Early Parental Depression," *Psychiatric Times*, June 2011.

INDEX

Health Insurance Reform Act
  (2010), 48
Herbal remedies, 18
Honikman, Jane, 81
Hoos, Michele, 22
Houston Chronicle (newspaper), 82

I
Income, prevalence of maternal
  depression by level of, *50*
Indoleamines, 32–33
Infanticide
  postpartum depression no excuse
    for, 87–92
  postpartum depression should be
    legal defense for, 80–86
  prevalence of, 90
  verdict on, *91*
Infants
  numbers born to depressed
    mothers, 52
  rates of parental depression by age
    of, *96*
  risks of mothers' use of
    antidepressants to, 59
Ingram, J., 49

K
Kendall-Tackett, Kathleen, 66
Khan, Arif, 56

L
Laney, Deanna, 84, 85
Law and Order (TV program), 88,
  92

Lithium, 23–24, 28
  risks of birth defects from, 25
Luvox. *See* Fluoxetine
Lykos, Pat, 85

M
Magnetic resonance imaging (MRI),
  41
McGuckin, Brian, 111
Medina, John J., 30
Melanie Blocker Stokes MOTHERS
  Act (2010), 47, 53–54, 59
Menendez, Robert, 54, *54*
Modarresi, Narjes, 80, 81, *82*, 83, 85–
  86
Monk, C., 49–50
Moses-Kolko, Eydie L., 41–42, 43
Mothers
  coping strategies for, 19
  depressed, prevalence of breast-
    feeding among, *72*
  emotional problems among
    married *vs.* unmarried, *42*
MOTHERS Act. *See* Melanie Blocker
  Stokes MOTHERS Act
MRI (magnetic resonance imaging),
  41

N
National Maternal and Infant
  Health Survey, US, 75
Neurosteroids, 35, 38
Neurotransmitters, 32–33
New Mothers Speak Out, 43
Newsweek (magazine), 90–91